CHARACTER AND
SOCIETY IN
SHAKESPEARE

CHARACTER AND SOCIETY IN SHAKESPEARE

BY

ARTHUR SEWELL

BYRON PROFESSOR OF ENGLISH LITERATURE
IN THE UNIVERSITY OF ATHENS

OXFORD
AT THE CLARENDON PRESS

Oxford University Press, Amen House, London E.C.4

GLASGOW NEW YORK TORONTO MELBOURNE WELLINGTON
BOMBAY CALCUTTA MADRAS KARACHI LAHORE DACCA
CAPE TOWN SALISBURY NAIROBI IBADAN ACCRA
KUALA LUMPUR HONG KONG

FIRST PUBLISHED 1951
REPRINTED LITHOGRAPHICALLY IN GREAT BRITAIN
AT THE UNIVERSITY PRESS, OXFORD
BY VIVIAN RIDLER, PRINTER TO THE UNIVERSITY
FROM SHEETS OF THE FIRST EDITION
1961

NOTE

PARTS of this essay had their original form in two short series of lectures delivered in the University of Athens during the Michaelmas Terms of 1949 and 1950. It has been considerably changed and added to for publication. I have to thank Dr. J. A. W. Bennett for reading it and commenting on it when it was in typescript.

A. S.

1951

CONTENTS

I. CHARACTER AND VISION   I

II. CHARACTER AND SOCIAL ORDER   38

III. THE MORAL DILEMMA IN TRAGEDY   53

IV. CHANGE IN THE TRAGIC CHARACTER   64

V. TRAGEDY AND 'THE KINGDOM OF ENDS'   91

VI. ORDER AND CONTINUANCE IN SOCIETY   122

INDEX OF NAMES   147

I

CHARACTER AND VISION

D R. JOHNSON once asked Kemble: 'Are you, sir, one of those enthusiasts who believe yourself transformed into the very character you represent?' When Kemble answered that 'he had never felt so strong a persuasion himself', Johnson said: 'To be sure not, sir, the thing is impossible. And if Garrick really believed himself to be that monster, Richard the Third, he deserved to be hanged every time he performed it.'

So far as the actor is concerned, most people would agree with Dr. Johnson. The art of the actor is the art of make-believe, but he induces belief in others, not in himself. The actor fashions the character with a sixth sense alert for what is going on in the audience. For him the intuition of the character and the presentation cannot be separated. The length of pause, the turn of a cadence, the momentum of a paragraph—these, and the raising of the hand, the step forward, the fixing of a stare, both create the character and present it; engage the collaboration of the audience and sustain the role. What emotion there is, is emotion recollected, not in tranquillity, but in excitement, the excitement of the theatre. And this applies even to the great Shakespearian roles. The actor who plays Hamlet sits quite still on his first appearance with the king and the court. He sits

B

still because, as Hamlet, he has nothing to say; but he also sits still, knowing, as actor, that silence is more effective than speech.

When we turn from the actor to the playwright, good authority would have us suppose that his case is quite different. Coleridge, for example, affirmed that Shakespeare was 'characterless', that he 'darted himself forth'. Keats, believing that the poet has no 'identity', wrote that Shakespeare was for ever 'in for and filling some other body'. A more modern and more elaborate statement of the same view takes advantage of psychoanalytical theory, as in this from Mr. J. I. M. Stewart: 'a man writes plays partly at least because he is beset by unexpressed selves; by the subliminal falling now into one coherent pattern and now into another of the varied elements of the total man.'

These good authorities seem to me to be in error. Certainly Shakespeare did not in this way 'dart himself forth' into all his characters. A humble analogy, perhaps, will illustrate this. When a child supposes himself to be a cowboy, he must also imagine for himself an Indian. To do this, he by no means becomes the Indian, and the Indian only has imaginary being so far as it is necessary for the child to be a successful cowboy. The Indian may, nevertheless, be a very 'real' Indian in the child's imagination: he may, indeed, be a younger brother. This childish make-believe is primitive drama, and it serves to illustrate the point that not all the characters in a play represent the 'unexpressed selves' by which the dramatist is 'beset'.

It is, surely, dangerous to equate character with 'self', or to suppose that to be acquainted with the character is to know much about the 'self'. To make this equation is to argue from the supposition that in every act the total self is engaged or that, if only we knew enough, we could deduce the total self from the particular act. Even if this were true in actual life (and I do not think it is), it is certainly not true in the fictive life of drama, and just as in actual life the self is very often no concern of ours in our dealings with other people, so in drama character is very often wholly unconcerned with self. The comic character, certainly, has no self, and ceases to be comic just so soon as we suppose him to be endowed with a self. The tragic character may be said to have a self, but this is by no means the self as the psychologists understand it; it is the moral self, which expresses itself in volition and is not to be usefully interpreted in terms of motivation.

To think of the playwright as being 'in for and filling some other body' is surely to misconceive the process of the dramatic imagination. A playwright imagines not only a character but also an actor. Very often, indeed, he has a particular actor or actress in mind, and this was true of Shakespeare. The available members of the acting profession have always had something to do with the invention of dramatic characters. Where a novelist will often use living 'models', the dramatist begins with a tradition of theatrical types, and his characters are much involved with modes of acting, conventions of elocution, and the like. The question, What sort of man

is this? is often asked by the dramatist in the form,
What sort of person will play this part and how is it to
be played? Aristotle recommended the playwright to
'go through the motions' so that his characters might
have verisimilitude. And the playwright may well do
this, but to 'go through the motions' is to play the part,
to imagine the actor and the audience.

Dramatic draughtsmanship—to create the character
in the round—is not concerned (except with the tragic
heroes, who, as we shall see, are a special case) with that
kind of actuality we have for ourselves but with the kind
of actuality other people have for us. Just as the *persona*
which the music-hall comedian creates is the product of
collaboration between himself and his audience, so it is
with many of Shakespeare's characters. What vitality
they have, and what consistency, does not come from
within but from without, and it is not 'depth psychology'
but a complex of social attitudes which gives them particular life. These characters have no private lives; they
live in public, before an audience. This is obviously true
about such a character as Launcelot Gobbo, but it is also
true of Iago and Falstaff. Iago has that kind of actuality
—and, except as a construction external to the play, no
more—which comes from an audience. In his soliloquies
he takes us into his confidence; he addresses us as though
our estimate of men might be the same as his. He takes
identity not from within but from without. Shakespeare
never 'darted himself forth' into Iago; he conceived
him, as the child-cowboy conceives the Indian, the
necessary antagonist to that other character, Othello,

who is conceived from within. Falstaff similarly has no private life. Falstaff must have his audience, and is, one may say, nobody when nobody is about. For, of course, we do not run away with Falstaff at Gadshill or counterfeit death at Shrewsbury; we watch him doing these things. It is almost true to say that while Shakespeare identified himself with Falstaff, as actor, he kept very much apart from him, as man. At most he does not assume the man; he assumes the attitude.

Some characters, notably the tragic heroes, seem certainly to be conceived from within, and an examination of the mode in which they are so conceived will form a major part of this essay. At this point of my argument, however, it is relevant to point out that while Shakespeare may have identified himself with these characters, the identification is never absolute. Shakespeare himself never becomes 'characterless'. We recognize Hamlet's problem as it appears to him; but how the problem appears to him never absolutely determines how it appears to us. His problem is known to us as his, not as ours, and although we look at the world through his eyes, it is we who look at the world. The apperception of a character, conceived from within—and, I do not doubt, the creation of that character—is something much more than vicarious experience. Further, even in so far as we may be said to be concerned with Hamlet's 'self', we are concerned with that self at the very point where psychology breaks down—at the point, namely, where the moral self takes on responsibility. The characteristic moment in Shakespeare's presentation of the tragic character is the moment at which that character, looking to the future, says, 'To be or not to be', or 'Now might I do it pat', or 'If it were done when 'tis done'; and this is the moment of moral responsibility, not psychological determination. It is, indeed, the moment when the character seeks to make some settlement in his moral encounter with the universe, not the moment in which the climax comes in a whole chain of psychological motivation. Character is very much more than is revealed in a case-history, and, perhaps, something less. In drama, as in ethics, psychology is still the handmaid, not the mistress.

II

The application of 'deep psychology' to character is at best plausible and ingenious, and has little to do with the presiding vision of the play. Mr. J. I. M. Stewart in his *Character and Motive in Shakespeare*, following an analysis by Freud, interprets Leontes' jealousy in *The Winter's Tale* as the projection upon Hermione of those homosexual desires which were awakened in him by Polixenes' actual presence for the first time since their 'twyn'd' boyhood. This hypothesis is a very good example of what this kind of speculation can do with character. For, assuming for a moment that it is a plausible hypothesis, what follows? The charge of homosexuality has been brought in to explain the situation and, as explanation, it lies outside the situation and is opaque to it. We do not know Leontes any the better after the charge has been made, and his treatment of Hermione is neither excused nor aggravated in our minds because of it. At the end of the play we suppose that Leontes is purged at the moment of repentance, but there is no trace of homosexuality in the evil of which he is purged. Such speculations should be seen for what they are; pretty—sometimes not so pretty—plays of the fancy with data sufficient for the pleasures of speculation but insufficient for the establishment of critical truth.

Sometimes, however, psychological inquiry may be accompanied by an obtuseness which blinds the critic to the fact that his probings into motivations are not only irrelevant to but plainly incompatible with the major vision of the play. Mr. Stewart himself warns us not to inquire too closely into the preceding events which might provide the external motivations for the situation in the play; as, for example, whether Macbeth and his wife have had previous talk of their conspiracy against the king. Shakespeare, Mr. Stewart says, has 'deliberately' left the matter confused, as a 'dramatic correlative' of the confusion in Macbeth's mind. Perhaps so. We should also be equally on our guard against searching out for deeper motivations which Shakespeare did not deliberately confuse but which he knew nothing about. To suggest that Leontes was involved in a homosexual fixation on his friend is to do far more artistic damage to the play than ever Bridges did to *Macbeth* when he suggested that Macbeth's motives were ambiguously presented. With Leontes (for how much of youth and age is there in *The Winter's Tale*?) innocence has been lost merely with the passing of the

years. In the darkness of an unspecified sense of guilt—
unspecified, because it is the common and puzzling case
of man—Leontes is so soured in his spirit that he projects
the general pollution upon Hermione and Polixenes.
To particularize his guilt and to focus the mind on
one specific way in which innocence might have been
lost is to change the perspective and distort all proper
emphasis. Who can read the Romances—even *The
Tempest*—and not say after Mr. Eliot, Do not let me
hear of the wisdom of old men!

III

There is little need to go to abnormal psychology
to explain the processes of dramatic composition. The
dramatist gives dramatic form to that dialectic through
which all of us, in our own way, seek to fashion—but
can never perfect—our address to the world. It is in the
greater range and comprehensiveness of this dialectic
that we discover what Keats termed Shakespeare's
'Negative Capability'. However great this range may
have been we must remember that the major argument
of dramatic composition is a positive argument, the
dramatist's unique way of looking at his world; this is
the presiding synthesis in which one character may be
seen (but the form is, of course, not triadic) as thesis,
another as antithesis.

This dialectic is expressed in the dramatic situation,
and a 'situation' is a relationship between characters,
involving volition and action, perhaps confined within
secular society, perhaps engaging the characters in that

larger relationship which men may have with God or the gods, and in which they are subject to a judgement more than the judgement of time. Action and volition are determined within the play not primarily by psychological motivation, but by those conflicting moral addresses to the universe which go to fashion the presiding vision. In poetic drama, at every moment, these conflicting moral addresses are transmuted into poetry, engaging the universe in words. The plays of Shakespeare discover for us two different but related activities, the one a kind of mimesis of the other. On one level, for example, Macbeth is apperceived as the tragic hero, caught in the net of his own making, giving himself to darkness, the prey of his own nightmares. But on another level, what engages us in the theatre as well as in the study is to hear and follow Macbeth, a poetic character, as he comes to terms with his dark universe in words, as he shapes for himself a poetic identity in language, in poetry. Just as costume at a fancy-dress ball may release our address to the world in a manner which seems to involve a metamorphosis of personality, so the situation makes the poet free to engage his universe on different terms, to deploy the constituent elements of his own personality in various ways, to make experiments, as it were, in ways of address to his world. The poetry of poetic drama is the poetry of 'As if', and the dramatist's 'As If' is made possible by the characters, and realizes itself in the situation.

Although the question we ask in drama is 'How ought men to address themselves to the world?' this question obviously involves the other question 'How do men so address themselves?' And it might seem that the answer to this question is best given by the psychologists, and indeed some scholars have recently suggested that with Shakespeare's characters the Elizabethan rather than the modern psychologist can help us here. And if we are to have one or the other, perhaps Elizabethan psychology can help us more. Elizabethan psychology was concerned with physiological causes chiefly as they determined the individual's approach and address to his world; and if Elizabethan psychology is relevant at all in our understanding of Shakespeare's characters its relevance lies more in the approach than in its causes. In the Elizabethan mind psychology had not yet been divorced from ethics and the two studies were, in fact, one. Modern psychological criticism in its stress on the question 'How do men approach their world and how is this approach motivated?' (as, for example, in Dr. Ernest Jones's *Hamlet and Oedipus*) by the very method of its inquiry takes the character out of the realm of morals into the realm of psychic determinism; and in this realm the character loses its dramatic, because it loses its moral, significance.

What then, is the place of 'deep psychology' in character-analysis? There are two possibilities. The psychologist may offer plausible explanations where a situation seems, on the face of it, difficult to understand or insufficiently motivated. He does this at his peril, for he may do artistic damage to the play, as we saw with Leontes in *The Winter's Tale*, or he may seek through over-subtlety to save the play for credibility, as many critics surely do in their account of the downfall of Angelo. In both these cases the psychological explanation seems to be superimposed on the character and is required not by the character, but by the situation. On the other hand, in certain situations which may perhaps be called 'archetypal', deep psychology may discover that secret impulses are involved which make that situation darker and perhaps more terrible in its importance to us. There is, for example, hardly a situation in the world's drama between mother and son in which it is improbable to detect, in the crisis of the relationship, something of what has come to be called the 'Oedipus complex'. Hamlet and Gertrude, Coriolanus and Volumnia, Oswald and Mrs. Alving, Orestes and Clytemnestra, Oedipus himself and Jocasta—all these relationships, in their crises, may well be deepened and darkened by the mysteries of the mother–son involvement. But we should remember that although Oedipus is involved in such a relationship of the utmost horror it was not character, so specified, that took him there. Nor can we explain Hamlet's delay in terms of the 'Oedipus complex'; although this 'complex' might well explain why this delay seems all the more painful to us. Hamlet's delay is not motivated by the fact that to kill the king would bring into the open long-suppressed and terrible desires; but its effect on us may be (if the analysis has validity at all) more powerfully moving because, in such a situation, such desires *might* be so revealed. This kind of analysis is to some extent analogous to the discovery of recondite ambiguities and depths in poetical imagery: but it often gives the same scope to mere ingenuity, and it should know its function.

IV

We can only understand Shakespeare's characters so long as we agree that we cannot know all about them and are not supposed to know all about them. They are real for us, but only real to the extent that we have an attitude towards them or make a judgement on them. This is not very different from the manner in which 'real' people are real for us, except that with 'real' people we bear in mind (if we are wise) that there is a great deal we do not know about them which might, if we knew it, change our attitude and our judgement. In this sense, attitude or judgement in the theatre are prior to 'character' and determine its actuality. What, for example, would happen to the play *Othello* if we could know that Iago, like Cassio, muttered in his dreams or could not sleep at nights? Are we certain, once we think of it, that this part of Iago's existence is excluded by anything other than the attitude we take towards him? We are not quite sure whether Iago really meant it when he said that he suspected Othello of having done his office in Emilia's bed; and the uncertainty arises partly from the fact that this is something we must not know about Othello, partly also from the fact that the inner feeling, involved in this, is something we must not know about Iago. There are 'rules of evidence' in drama just as there are in a court of law.

Our attitudes may, indeed, survive evidence quite hostile to them, if that evidence conflicts with other designs made on our partialities or sympathies. We can sometimes be as unfair as a crowd at a football match when the home team is losing. Bassanio is a Venetian gentleman and we approve of his match with Portia; but evidence would set him down as a fortune-hunter who borrows money from his friend and allows him to sign a fatal bond. Henry V's royalty all but makes us overlook—or try to explain away—his treatment of Falstaff. Mr. T. S. Eliot, with characteristic impassivity, has said that he still awaits an answer to Thomas Rymer, who found in *Othello* no more than a blackamoor who had made a foolish marriage, and a recommendation to wives to look well to their linen. In saying this, Mr. Eliot has perhaps taken too much notice of evidence that is inadmissible.

It was surely a mistake ever to ask the question: Is Falstaff a coward? Morgann, who first asked it, very rightly made the distinction between the Understanding, which deals in actions, and the Impression made upon us, often at variance with the Understanding. Morgann also affirmed of character-presentation that 'just so much is shewn as is requisite, just so much as is impressed': but he went on to say that this 'just so much' is able to imply a character which, though 'seen in part', may yet be 'capable of being unfolded and understood as a whole'. He therefore believed it possible to answer the question and proper to put it: Is Falstaff a coward? One might answer that the facts say that he is, but our impression of him, our attitude to him, says that he is not. Falstaff ran away, pretended to be dead; and to do these things was to put the safety of his skin above his human dignity, and this might be thought to be a sort of 'cowardice'. But not when we are dealing with Falstaff, for Falstaff was very doubtful about 'honour', and if we do not believe in 'honour' the word 'cowardice' has no meaning. Falstaff is not to be judged, as a real person might be judged, in terms of the ordinary moral categories. His running away, his pretending to be dead, his speech on 'honour' are all part of his attitude to his world, and it is this that calls from us the ambiguous, even face-saving, judgement of laughter. We do not ask, Was Falstaff a coward? just because we are ourselves infected with Falstaff's notion that perhaps, after all, the question is not so important as we thought it was.

Falstaff is a character, not a real person. What wholeness and consistency he has comes not from within but from the address of his personality *vis-à-vis* his world as it transforms itself into speech and behaviour. The world is his stooge and, so magnanimously does he present himself, he is his own stooge. He subdues and transforms the matter of the moment—even his own monstrous belly—to the purposes of his superlatively comic vision. Such a representation of personality is to be found in a work of art, and its consistency is not psychological but aesthetic. It is the notable distinction of Falstaff's being that he has been conceived quite independently of psychological motivation. His delights, like ours, are aesthetic, even though they have their play in the uncertain world of our moral scruples.

V

Falstaff is aware of his audience, on and off the stage, and the comic artistry is part of the comic character. His life within the play—the only life he has—is a sustained vaudeville turn. The audience is necessary to his being. Nor is he alone of Shakespeare's characters in this. In these characters—they are as various as the melancholy Jaques, Iago, Richard III, Autolycus—we seem to have a high degree of self-awareness which would argue that identification of himself with the character which Coleridge and Keats attributed to Shakespeare. The truth is, however, that in the creation of these persons Shakespeare's identification of himself is not with the character but with the actor. And this identification does not make him ask, What does it feel like to be Falstaff, Iago, Jaques, Richard III? but rather, What effect is Falstaff, Iago, Jaques, Richard III, to make on his audience? A very different matter. This effect is the product of an address to the world, here and now made concrete in the address to the audience.

Each one of these characters has something of the detachment of the artist, and each achieves a satisfaction which has in it an element predominantly aesthetic. From moment to moment they seem to generate a mimesis of their own personalities, and only in the mimesis is the personality really known. They address our moral attitudes and sensibilities, as an artist does,

taking their licence for granted, such licence they
must have. With them, as with the artist, we give (often
through laughter) a temporary permission to a view of
life, a questioning of moral conventions, an affirmation
of cynical assessments, which—if our neighbour pressed
us on the matter—we might well reject. Not only is dis-
belief in the theatre willingly suspended, but also moral
scruples and even accustomed decencies. Both kinds of
suspension are necessary to the presentation of character.

This suspension is, of course, never absolute. We give
licence as a nobleman may license his fool. We keep our
moral scruples and our decencies safely in reserve.
Nevertheless, when the character addresses us, he is
making a bid for our assent that his attitude, his moral
outlook, is more rational than ours. He comes to us, and
he asks: 'Who is it, then, that says I play the villain?'

VI

Drama, then, through character, prompts us to say:
So that is what the world is like, is it? And this or that
is the way in which I am recommended to act in my
approach to the world? For, after all, vision is not wholly
divorced from persuasion. Just as important, perhaps, in
the formulation of vision as the way in which certain
characters approach their world, is the way in which
the world makes its impact on men and women despite
themselves. Character, properly understood, is discovered not only in what men do to the world, but also
in what the world does to them. The character of
Charlie Chaplin, for example, was largely determined

by the fact that whenever he trod on another man's toe, that man would be at least twice his size. That was the world not so much as he viewed it but as he experienced it. It was his world, despite himself. Our attitude to a character—that is, the way in which the character becomes actual for us—is determined very often not by what the character does or says but by what happens to him. Desdemona and Ophelia are, in part, the creatures of our compassion; Cordelia's kind suffers and dies young. Gloucester takes on a distinction not hitherto his own when his eyes are plucked out and he goes blind from the castle. Romeo and Juliet are what they are very much because their names were elected for misfortune.

What happens to a person may, in this sense, be just as much 'in character' or 'out of character' as what the person says or does, and the very probabilities of the play are determined by our attitudes. With Kent, we feel that Lear must die because we would not 'on the rack of this rough world stretch him out longer'. But we are embarrassed when the king dismisses Falstaff, because our attitude to Falstaff has never included the expectation that his spirits could be so put down. Similarly, the indignities heaped upon Malvolio are almost more than the character can bear.

VII

There are in character many kinds of actuality, and they derive in different modes; but all these modes are involved in our vision of our world and our evaluation

of that world. The consistency of the character, like its
significance, is generated within our moral attitudes.
Unless Shakespeare had set our minds busy—and not
only our minds—on various kinds of evaluation, his
characters could never have engaged us and would
have lacked all vitality:

> ... no man is the lord of anything,
>   Though in and of him there be much consisting,
>   Till he communicate his parts to others.

This is true in a special sense of dramatic characters. One
character may come to us affirming his own scale of
values, setting it up in competition with ours. Another,
even a poor stooge in man's traffic with man, will
serve involuntarily that transformation of moral vision
into dramatic form which is the primary business of the
dramatist. That vision may concern itself with secular
morality; it may concern itself with what buffeting the
world may mete out to a man; but it may also deal with
man's ultimate predicament, his ultimate worth, his
status in the universe. Sometimes, as in comedy, our
social and moral assurances are ruffled and then as-
suaged; but at other times, in the great tragedies, the
darker and more secret securities of the spirit are deeply
disturbed or made serene.

Drama does not merely give scope to unacted desires;
it acts and judges them; and the judgement is in the act
of vision. Just as Coleridge could believe that the variety
of Nature is, as it were, the other side of Mind, Mind
getting to know itself, so we may suppose that the variety

of characters in Shakespeare's plays is the other side of Shakespeare's vision, vision getting to know itself. And, in the deepest sense of the word, the vision is primarily moral.

VIII

In Ben Jonson's comedies (in *Volpone*, for example) the characters are directly deduced from Jonson's way of looking at the world, from his moral vision. They are no more (and no less) than the products of that vision. It is significant, perhaps, that in *Volpone*, as in Jonson's other astringent comedy, *The Alchemist*, there is one character who seems to be entirely self-aware (like Richard III or Iago) and who takes an aesthetic delight, so it would seem, in subjecting the matter and situation of the moment to the transforming exercise of his personality. In a sense, Corbaccio, Voltore, and Corvino are Volpone's creations, his stooges, perhaps in something the same way as he is Jonson's, making a kind of hierarchy of character-creation—although Moscha does not fit quite so easily into the pattern. Volpone uses these characters to substantiate his address to the world—just as Jonson uses him.

Nothing, perhaps, is as simple as this in Shakespeare. He has his absolute stooges in the earlier plays, but later he is so copious in invention and in vision that even his stooges have a way of coming to life, of becoming for a moment in themselves a unique, if partial, fulfilment of that vision. And so, in Shakespeare's plays, the essential process of character-creation is a prismatic breaking-up of the comprehensive vision of the play;

and each element of vision, so separated out, is in itself a unique illumination, finding its individual fulfilment in character.

Whereas, in *Volpone*, a character like Corbaccio mainly extends and elaborates the vision which is wholly implicit in Volpone himself, in Shakespeare's mature plays even a minor character will enrich, diversify, and individually quicken the comprehensive view. Of that view he is the product, but in that view he is also an agent. The minor character is not merely a deduction from the theme of the play, related by a kind of dramatic geometry to the whole pattern. In him, as in a single brush-stroke in a picture, a moment of vision, a new angle of attitude, transforms to however small an extent, and lights up, the whole matter.

So it is with Barnardine in *Measure for Measure*, who refuses to be hanged because he has been drinking all night, and is not 'fitted for it'. In that moment we behold, in a different light, all those things the play is about—authority, the law, due procedure, even mercy —and, like Barnardine, we behold them unabashed. In a manner possible only to his comprehensive soul, Shakespeare (as with the brush-stroke in the picture) has transformed and more subtly defined the total vision of the play.

Thus, too, in *Antony and Cleopatra* we see through Cleopatra a world in which sensuality is for us a 'mystery' —not, as Mr. J. I. M. Stewart suggests, a 'mystery' for Cleopatra herself, for there is something a little absurd in supposing that, together with the priests, she blesses

herself when she is 'riggish'. Of that same world, however, Charmian, Iras, and Alexas are also part, and in
them sensuality is not a 'mystery' but something quite
different, and yet Cleopatra moves in their company,
a royal figure. This same world, too, we see as Enobarbus
sees it, when he says, 'Mine, and most of our fortunes
tonight, shall be—drunk to bed.' Each contributes to
our vision of a world in which sensuality might be a
'mystery' and might, too, be no mystery at all; and this
vision is only part of the total vision of the play, which
comprehends the austerities of Rome as well as the
ardours of Egypt.

IX

The character's address to the world—which involves
also the way in which we apprehend him in relation to
the world, and, perhaps, the kind of world in which
he is so apprehended—may sometimes be expressed by
the simple device of self-explanation. Shakespeare uses,
from time to time, a simple expository presentation of
character. There are, however, two kinds of exposition
—one in which the character is presented or presents
himself in general relation to the world and to society,
and the other in which the character is presented or
presents himself merely in terms of the facts and feelings
of the particular situation. In the one case we see the
world because of and through the character, but the
effect may be rarefied because there is no dramatic con-
centration in the imagining of the character. In the
other case the effect may be limited and even bombastic,

because there has been no generalizing exercise of the imagination. An ideal form of character-presentation in poetic drama is that in which from moment to moment the character is realized within the particular situation and from that situation through him is distilled and concentrated poetic truth.

A character, nevertheless, like a model sitting for the photographer, has to be *posed*, and self-exposition is one way in which Shakespeare gets the character, as it were, into position. He does this with Antonio in *The Merchant of Venice* with his 'In sooth, I know not why I am so sad', and in *Twelfth Night* with the Duke and his 'If music be the food of love'. Edmund's 'This is the excellent foppery of the world' and Iago's 'Thus do I ever make my fool my purse'—and here the device goes a stage farther—get the characters into position not only in relation to their world but also in relation to their audience. In this way, then, we see the soliloquy, from one point of view, as a device by which Shakespeare settles and re-settles the disposition of his character in relation to his world and in relation to his audience.

A character is known most poignantly when from within the particular situation he directs our vision to the more general world. When Lear's mind turns to the 'poor naked wretches' he becomes more actual for us just because the 'poor naked wretches' are so actual for us, and they are actual because it is he, Lear, of all people in this world, who at this moment thinks of them. This is, indeed, particular personality distilled into poetry, the essence of poetic drama. And when this kind

of distillation fails Shakespeare's achievement is something less. So, in *Hamlet*, I have always felt that the
soliloquy beginning:

> O what a rogue and peasant slave am I,

though very often spoken effectively by the actor, has in
it the element of bombast, as though the matter of the
moment has not submitted to poetic treatment. It is not
a speech in which, by the persuasion of poetry, our
vision is directed to the general predicament of man,
or in which that general predicament is known more
intensely because of Hamlet's case. Vision in *Hamlet*
may be thought, indeed, to be too often the findings
of Hamlet's 'melancholy' and too rarely the discovery,
through poetry, of what is general in his particular case.
In poetic drama incident and situation are, or should
be, catalysts by means of which, in character, vision is
released, embodied, and enriched.

x

When a dramatic character addresses his world, he
also addresses us—the audience. We are that world, and
if the address does not make its impact on us we are
likely to miss it. We are the sounding-board. Concreteness in character-creation, then, must result, to some
extent, from the liveliness with which the person of the
play establishes some kind of *rabport* with his audience—
for the audience is something more than a collection of
eavesdroppers. The main difference between Mercutio
and Romeo (except in Romeo's fight with Tybalt,

where an audience demands his attention) is that Mercutio lives and dies, acting, and Romeo does not. The audience give life to Mercutio even when he is dying, but Romeo might very often just as well be talking for the stars.

To establish a *rapport* with his audience a character must use a dramatic speech which not merely has in it the accents of actuality but also lends itself to that subtle control of the audience's affections which is a large part of the art of the actor. This *rapport*—and with it, the character—disappears when language is literary rather than dramatic, when figures are extended for their own sakes, when speech-rhythm is too closely controlled by the metre. The development of Shakespeare's verse is certainly towards a handling of metre which gives greater flexibility to the accent of naturalistic speech; but this must not be thought of simply as the result of a more subtle and lively realization of character, for it is equally the result of a more subtle and lively presentation of character to an audience. Verse loses the accents of speech, when the dramatist forgets the audience, as much as when he forgets the character. Indeed, since creation and presentation of character are one and the same business, to forget the audience is to forget the character. So it is that, in the early plays, the persons who belong to the theatre and find there their absolute climate—the Dromios, Launce, the Nurse, Launcelot—speak a natural accent, come to life, and make us laugh. Other characters have not yet made the theatre their particular home.

Such characters 'come to life'. But what kind of life do they have?

The servants in Shakespeare's early plays were doubtless played by well-known comic actors, who could, like Tarleton, put their faces through the curtain and set the whole house laughing. Launce, with his little dog, is really a creature of the vaudeville stage, and so is Launcelot Gobbo. With these characters we enjoy that kind of dramatic suspense which wonders what the player is going to say next, what new impertinence will make us laugh.

Comic characterization of this kind depends, in fact, on certain devices of verbal usage. Speech is the principal medium of coherence in society, the mark of class and status, the instrument by which men live in community. If speech habits and expectations are disturbed, something of order in society is put into jeopardy. And when a comic person, of the servant type, makes puns, chops logic, comes to syllogistic conclusions, uses language above his station, as Shakespeare's servants often do, we argue the character, as a sort of hypostatization, from that play upon our social attitudes which is involved in the application of certain verbal forms to matter unsuited to them. The disrespectful attitude to language is a disrespectful attitude to social order. What we call 'character' is really no more than a by-product of the dramatic purpose, which was a certain comic play upon our social attitudes. There is a sense in which we can say that, in so far as these comic persons are involved in the matter of the comedy, they treat that

matter merely as material for comic art; and character,
in this particular form at least, is no more than a humble
analogy for what we call personality in a work of art.
Character is discovered in the same way as personality
is discovered, say, in the familiar essay. To indulge in
the 'personal heresy' in the study of this kind of characterization has no more relevance than in literary criticism—no more and no less.

XI

Perhaps we can find a better analogy. Dr. Johnson, as
we know him from Boswell, so transforms his personality into talk that talk is for him almost an art-form.
From Boswell we know a good deal of Dr. Johnson's
personal appearance and habits. His gait was rolling;
he was blind in one eye; he was like a bear at a party.
And all this is something. But there is another Dr. Johnson—or the same man known differently—out of whom
all these matters of fact have been filtered, or rendered
into the substance of talk; a Dr. Johnson whose talk to
the Club is his address to the universe, and into whose
talk the gait, the semi-blindness, the scrofulosity, even
the dirty linen are all transubstantiated, so that they
come out as prejudice and common sense and compassion and fear of death. It may be said of Dr. Johnson
that when he was talking he was most himself; and this
is true of Shakespeare's characters.

XII

If character is chiefly discovered for us in the mode
in which the person of the play embodies in prose or

poetry a distinctive address to the world, we should expect that something of that address will show itself in imagery, vocabulary, tone of speech, style, peculiar to that person. To substantiate this view would involve an examination of Shakespeare's imagery and versification, hitherto little attended to—how far are the imagery and versification distinctive in the various persons of the play?

The character will reveal in words the world familiar to him and his address to that world; but, in addition, as he presents the character, Shakespeare must have mediated between the fictive personality and the speech in which he discovers him, so that this speech will be determined partly by the fictive personality itself and partly by the poetical mode of presentation. Clearly, for example, Hotspur's personality is rendered in the verse assigned to him by a kind of mimesis, so that his words in their momentum, their rhythm, and the range of their associations contain and express the very behaviour of his spirit as Shakespeare sought to present it.

We may say, indeed, that the presentation of character in poetic drama is to some extent akin to and involved with what we call 'style'. If character is very often disclosed much as personality is disclosed in a work of art, we should expect that the stylistic elements of language will be engaged in the process of embodiment. Because Iago's world-view is more confined, more logical, less fluid than Othello's, we should expect him to contain his meaning more often within the line, to use a linear rhythm rather than a paragraphic, to speak with a more mathematical preciseness than Othello. And this is exactly what we find. We must not look, then, so much for a merely naturalistic imitation of idiosyncrasies in speech; although, of course, Shakespeare sometimes used this in his earlier plays. We look rather for that distillation of personality into style which is unmistakable in characters as early as Mercutio and the Bastard. That the successful achievement of this kind of style presupposes the appropriateness of the verse for dramatic speech is not evidence of a naturalistic conception of character but a necessary accommodation to the medium of the theatre and the voice of the actor.

To consider imagery more particularly. In a recent article in *Shakespeare Survey II* Mr. Mikhail M. Morozov wrote:

> If . . . we should find definite laws governing the imagery of the individual characters we shall thereby, first, again confirm the fact that Shakespeare's characters do not speak for the author but, so to say, 'for themselves', i.e. are independent individuals (in other words we shall obtain new confirmation of Shakespeare's *realism*).

It is, perhaps, a little unfair to point out—for Mr. Morozov's analyses are helpful—that one example of this 'realism' is the inference that 'Iago was probably once a sailor' because he uses a certain number of naval images. But the example serves to show the dangers involved in an analysis which begins with the supposition that 'Shakespeare's characters do not speak for the author but, so to say, for themselves'.

We must inquire a little more closely how, in fact,

character is individualized in imagery; remembering that, if words are to keep their meanings, the characters do more truly 'speak for the author' than 'for themselves'. To create a character is to imagine an individual address to the world, but to imagine such an address involves also the imagining of a world—not a world specified by matters of fact, but a world of quality in which each matter of fact is something more than accidental. A mode of vision, an attitude to life, is rendered in poetic speech. Hotspur declares it 'an easy leap to pluck bright honour from the pale-faced moon', and in this Shakespeare gives us a poetical epitome of Hotspur's characteristic behaviour. But *realism* is altogether abrogated here, and if Hotspur does not speak for the author at least, through Hotspur, the author speaks for Hotspur. We do not question the credibility of the speech, because Shakespeare has found a poetic equivalent for that address to life which we may suppose to be implicit in Hotspur's behaviour. The poetic equivalent, however, is Shakespeare's and not Hotspur's, and carries in itself its own comment, even its own irony.

Character is individualized in imagery, because imagery creates the world as the character apprehends it and appropriates it—or rather, as the author imagines, in one activity, the character and the world as that character perceives it. Indeed, the matter is less straightforward even than this. For the language the character speaks is very often the poetic equivalent of his 'nature'; and his 'nature' is his characteristic address to the world, and this is nothing but the manner in which he discovers and engages his world in speech. But the poetic equivalent is generated by the dramatist within the situation. In all this, what we are really affirming is that there is no prose rendering for the poetically-conceived character, just as the paraphrase is never the poetry.

XIII

Othello and Iago in this way characterize by their imagery the worlds they engage and in which they live. It may, indeed, be suggested at the outset that there is a certain important difference in the manner in which these worlds are affirmed. Othello's world is dynamic and he is, in a sense, the creative centre of it. He creates his world from moment to moment, and it may be said in him that Mind and Nature are one. Iago, on the other hand, lives in a static world, in which men's characters are catalogued and their behaviours predicted. Othello's is a perceptual, Iago's a conceptual universe. This difference marks, as we shall see, a profound difference in the function they fulfil in the vision of their author; for imagery characterizes not only that world to which the persons address themselves but also the kind of world to which that address is made and the mode of vision in which that address is comprehended.

In Iago's world everything is catalogued from observation. No image seems to have passed through his being, there to have been forged and fused. He has, as Mr. Morozov notes, a very large number of images of beasts; but these images are no more than emblems of men's weaknesses and vices. When he refers to Othello as an 'old black ram' this is smoking-room or barrack-room talk; it has nothing in common with Othello's 'Goats and monkeys!' His images very often, too, come, as do his judgements, from social behaviour and, with what emotional force there is behind them, reinforce these judgements.

> You shall mark
> Many a duteous and knee-crooking knave
> That, doting on his own obsequious bondage,
> Wears out his time, much like his master's ass,
> For naught but provender; and when he's old, cashiered.

Such images illustrate both the idea and the emotion—and that is their function; they have none of the enrichment of fruitful ambiguity.

Iago rarely reveals a present emotion. His images always *refer to* an emotion of old standing, never generate the emotion in the moment, from the centre. Except at the end he has no present discomfitures, no present excitements. He is never in doubt. Consequently he can, as it were, move out of the time of the play, especially in his soliloquies, in a way impossible to Othello. He can, and to all intents and purposes does, speak about himself in the third person, as though he should take the audience into his confidence and say: 'You and I know this Iago well enough, but they can't catch him, not this poor trash of Venice, this nigger and this silly girl. Iago is much too fly for them.' Inevitably language which is not caught and contained within the concrete *time* of the play employs a different kind of imagery, less particular, more external. A less external, more particular kind of image would, in fact, misrepresent him. He addresses himself—and so must his language—to each situation as steadily as a compass to its pole.

It must be clear from what precedes that it is not only the *provenance* of the images that individualizes character but also their form and their activity.

Othello's world, which he creates in his imagery, is not at all the social world in which Iago has his being. There are, except as objects abstractly recognized, no heavens, no oceans, in the world of Iago. Othello's world is the universe itself, which he all but creates, where the sun and the moon at his imagining suffer their huge eclipses, where heaven and hell are in their places, where vast seas wash the shores, and oceans meet each other. When Iago calls on his world:

> Take note, take note, O world!
> To be direct and honest is not safe,

he means the world of men. But when a few lines later Othello uses the same word, the 'world' becomes as large as its history, and contains both seas and continents:

> By the world,
> I think my wife be honest and think she is not—

so different are the worlds which they address. Iago's is a pragmatic world, and his imagery finds its authority in social usage. Othello's world is the poetical aggrandizement of himself, and as he addresses he creates it.

While Iago, being a character statically conceived,

must necessarily be, as it were, external to the imagery he uses, Othello's nature is in every word. We might say that imagery illustrates and elaborates Iago's character; but it creates Othello's. In his speech words come active from those deeps of language in which they return to their early origin and are reinforced in their primitive energies. The living image comes out of the chrysalis of the concept and takes on unique being. And whereas in Iago's soliloquies time is external to language and no more than time taken to utter the words, in Othello's speeches time is very often transformed and becomes the dimension of the living language itself, as it creates its own space in its own time. Do we not feel, for example, that in the famous temptation scene Iago lives not so much in the dimension of his own time as in Othello's? Or, perhaps, is there not here a subtle interplay between two kinds of time, as I believe there to be in *King Lear* when Lear and the fool are out in the storm? This interplay of two kinds of time, indeed, seems to me symbolical of a deeper interplay, which is part of the business of tragedy; and this interplay has its concrete representation, is made external, through the processes of language.

XIV

There is one small point to add here to what has been said of the relation between imagery and character. Imagery has a great deal to do with tone in character-presentation, and this is a very important element, certainly for the actor. Mr. Morozov notes that Hamlet's

images are very often 'close to the heart of the common element' and must have 'endeared [him] to the
popular audience'. This is surely true. Hamlet should
be played as a warmer, a more sympathetic figure than
is common in modern stage interpretations. He has in
him something of the coarseness, even the brutality,
which marks Mercutio—and Iago; and his images
reveal it. I do not pursue the point; but it is very easy
to recognize the change in tone in the presentation of
Ophelia after she has gone mad.

XV

The view of character here put forward seems to take
little account of the fact that Shakespeare's characters
awaken in us emotions of pity, contempt, admiration,
loathing, and the like, and that in this they can be
fruitfully thought of as very real persons. Once we deny
in tragedy, for example, our pity for this man's mis-
fortunes, our admiration for some grandeur in his soul,
what is left? Is drama really so bloodless that we go to
the theatre to become acquainted with a pattern of life-
views? In comedy, do we not rejoice that a man has
been caught in his folly and has been chastened? In
tragedy, do we not witness the spectacle of a man, a particular man, at odds with his fate?

It is the experience of many of us, I fancy, that in the
theatre or in the cinema—perhaps after a very good
dinner—we have sat with a lump in our throats and
tears welling just beneath our eyelids, devoutly hoping
that the lights will not go up too soon. Cheap drama,

like cheap music, can be curiously potent. And the reason for this seems to be that we are moved by the spectacle of what is happening to this man, this particular man—there, in front of us!—because there is nothing else for us to concern ourselves about. We are at the mercy of the simple stimulus. We are overwhelmed by the tearful situation, because the imagination and the intellect are not otherwise engaged. For the moment, we are debauched.

In Shakespeare's plays, however, what pity we feel, what terror, is of quite a different kind. The stimulus is by no means simple. We have a great deal else to concern ourselves about. And very often, when something like actuality, perhaps unbidden, breaks through, we are at a loss. We become, in fact, at the mercy of the simple stimulus.

I believe that this happens in Shakespeare's final dealings with Falstaff in *Henry IV, Part II*. In general the truly comic character, *qua* comic character, has no interior mode of existence, and what he feels has no relevance in our attitude towards him. Who asks what Falstaff is *feeling*, when he runs away at Gadshill, or counterfeits death at Shrewsbury? Who cares? Are his knees knocking? Do his limbs tremble? Does his heart miss a beat, except for the unusual exercise? Who asks these questions? But, in the end, when the king rejects him, questions of this sort must be asked. At that moment —all the attempts to excuse the king prove this point— we are compelled to ask: What is Falstaff feeling about all this? At last he is brought up to it—a situation which he cannot turn to his own comic purposes, intractable as it is to the subduing magic of personality, his address to the world. This address had never had to reckon with such a moment, and, for the moment, it is quite put down. We are a little ashamed of ourselves. The Falstaff we knew has never asked for our pity. We can do no more than fumble with our sympathies, tell ourselves that it had to be, bear in mind Henry V, justify (or condemn) the king that acts so. And all this because without the transforming power profanity, old age, and surfeit-swelling are no other than themselves, and we had thought them otherwise. We have to treat Falstaff—with what loss!—as a real person. We pity this fat old man; but we cannot say 'The pity of it!' And it is only when we pity and can also say, enlarging the moment in its significance, 'The pity of it!' that pity is more than self-indulgence. Unless what happens to the character is a mode of bringing together into more poignant relationship the character's way of meeting his world and the comprehensive vision of the play, the character becomes no other than a 'real person', and we may be affected more, but moved less. The emotion, like the incident which arouses it, should be a catalyst by means of which vision is released and enriched, so that the particular case is apprehended in terms of the general case of Man.

We suffer something of the same kind of embarrassment in the discomfiture of Shylock and Malvolio.

A different but equally interesting case is found in *Two Gentlemen of Verona*. It is the rule in comedy that characters shall run true to type, that they should behave according to their 'humours', that we should know where we are with them. When Proteus, friend of Valentine and lover of Julia, discovers his new affection for Silvia, Valentine's lady, we are presented with a moral crisis outside the realm of the particular comic vision. Proteus loses identity, becomes no more than a 'real person', and we do not know what to make of him. The moral crisis, so posed, is prose sediment in the poetry, and the judgement we must make on Proteus is a prose judgement, having nothing to do with the poetry.

II

CHARACTER AND SOCIAL ORDER

I PROPOSE now to examine some of the implications of these views in our reading of the plays, treating separately comedy, history, tragedy, and 'Romance'. Before I do this, however, it is necessary to make some general observations on the kinds of address to the world that a character may make, and on the kinds of reception the world may give to that address. These kinds, of course, are corollaries of each other.

A character's address to the world determines the world in which the address is made and in terms of which the character is to be apperceived. The major distinction which we may make among such worlds is between one contained in time and one which transcends time. In other words, the universe to which the character may be supposed to accommodate himself may be a universe of physical happenings and secular judgements, or it may be a universe in which the physical and the metaphysical march together and in which the secular judgement no longer has supreme relevance. It is not always easy to say, perhaps, how the world 'around the corner' is implied or affirmed in the presentation of character—Mr. T. S. Eliot, for example, taking the manner and the design of drawing-room comedy in *The Cocktail Party*, succeeds in doing it, and

Ibsen, in *Hedda Gabler*, endows the neurotic restlessness of a middle-class wife with significances which give tragic impressiveness to the vulgarities of commonplace frustration. In *The Cocktail Party*, whether in the drawing-room or in the consulting-room, we know that there are some souls will be saved and some souls will not be saved, and in *Hedda Gabler*, in that over-furnished parlour, we know that Hedda is subject to a judgement which neither Tesman nor his aunts can understand.

We ourselves co-operate in making this distinction by the attitude we take, and by the way in which we confine or enlarge the universe in which we apprehend the character presented. To put the matter very simply, we might say that there are occasions in the theatre when we ask the questions, What does speech and behaviour of this sort do to society? How do we, as members of secular society, receive what is being transacted before us? There are other occasions when we ask the question, What does this character do to himself? And we ask this question because, whatever our formulated beliefs, there is a level on which both we and the character belong to a society no longer secular and on which what happens to him is also something that happens to us, and his guilt, his suffering, his tragedy, are ours, for in this society we are members of each other. And it is on this level that we both 'dart ourselves forth' and remain ourselves; for our 'identification' with the character is not psychological but moral; we do not 'fill some other body', we experience the moral community of mankind.

XVII

All Shakespeare's characters seem to have been conceived in terms of some kind of order. Order, as Dr. Tillyard has pointed out, was a pervading notion in Shakespeare's day, and Shakespeare himself makes many references to it. It is in its effect on *order*, of whatever kind, that a character's address to the world is apprehended. It is in his place in some kind of order that the character is recognized. Othello's cry, 'And when I love thee not, Chaos is come again', gives us the clue to the presiding idea in Shakespeare's creation of character. Order and disorder—social, political, moral—are the poles between which the characters move.

I am concerned in this section to illustrate this, in its relation to the treatment of comic characters, from *The Merchant of Venice*. We shall there discover the mode in which, in one of the comedies, the comprehensive vision of the play presides over the presentation of character.

In the first scene of *The Merchant of Venice* the presentation of characters in their social setting is much more important than their individualization. Every image in Salarino's first speech—for it is mainly in imagery that the idea of order is particularized—is an image drawn from a special area of social experience. The argosies become 'signiors and burghers', or 'pageants'; the rise and fall of the tall ships are likened to 'curtsies', and social ranking is implied in the phrase 'do them reverence'. It is a short speech which settles us in an acceptance of this ordered and opulent society. Then

Salanio takes up the tale and, in a different manner, he sustains the same effect. For the kind of conduct he pictures—the plucking of the grass to know where the wind sits; the anxious peering into maps—is the technical business of men in an organized economy, where the system of distribution and production depends on an ordered knowledge of natural conditions. And later, when Antonio answers that it is none of the hazards of commerce that makes him sad, we become acquainted with that necessary prudence which makes our economies safe:

> My ventures are not in one bottom trusted,
> Nor to one place;

Whereat, Antonio's denial sets Salarino off dividing men into two classes, according to their *social* behaviour: those who laugh they know not why and those who never laugh at all.

Even a chance word contributes to the picture, as when Antonio says to Salarino,

> I take it, your own business calls you . . .,

where the meaning of the word 'business' is particularized in the context which has previously made mention of 'argosies' and 'signiors' and 'burghers'.

A little later Bassanio unfolds his plan of going to seek Portia at Belmont, and he makes known his need of money for this purpose. He is a gentleman. He has some right in birth and station, we must believe, to show

> a more swelling port
> Than my faint means would grant continuance.

Commercial society applauds his determination to get rid of his debts and aristocratic society has never condemned a gentleman for entering into matrimony to mend his fortunes. Gallant society likes the reminiscence of the manly sports of his earlier days, and is prepared to condone his 'wilful youth', since the sowing of wild oats is a guarantee against worse disorder. Besides, since society knows that it is woman who, in Coleridge's phrase, 'continuates society', it admires the language in which Portia is praised. The match is, socially speaking, wholly desirable.

We very soon become aware of a nice arrangement of social ranking in the play—as with Portia and Nerissa, Bassanio and Gratiano. And there are clear indications that abnormalities of birth and station will disqualify men from an open passport to social relationships. Shylock is a Jew and has dealings with the Venetians; but he says:

I will buy with you, sell with you, talk with you, walk with you, and so following; but I will not eat with you, drink with you, nor pray with you.

Nor, in general, they with him. Jessica is a Jewess, but society can accept her, married to Lorenzo and turned Christian. The Prince of Morocco is black, or he might have passed:

A gentle riddance—Draw the curtains, go;
May all of his complexion choose me so.

It is a society which has its ideals of polite behaviour. Bassanio must go to Belmont with his baggage full of presents, even though he has to borrow the money to pay for them. The suitors, whom Portia would reject, are so rejected because they fall short of social approbation. She rejects them, just as at another time she might be unwilling to ask them to afternoon tea. The Neapolitan is a bore, and talks of nothing but his horse. The Englishman is 'a proper man's picture', but he has no languages and is 'a dumb show'. The German is usually drunk. Bassanio, on the other hand, is altogether acceptable. He is a Venetian gentleman, a scholar, and a soldier. He came once in the company of a marquis. He is 'best deserving a fair lady' and 'worthy of praise'.

Social order depends on the fulfilment of social obligations, and *The Merchant of Venice* is a play greatly concerned with the contractual relations between men and men. There is an element of contract in almost every detail of the plot: the Jew's bond with Antonio, the will of Portia's father, the suitor's pledge to fulfil the terms of the will, the release of Launcelot from his obligations to Shylock, the pledge accompanying the gift of rings. The effect of these contractual elements is continually reinforced by the mention of oaths.

> The Prince of Aragon hath ta'en his oath.

>   I could teach you
> How to choose right, but then I am forsworn.

> I have toward Heaven breathed a sacred vow
> To live in prayer and contemplation.

> By yonder moon, I swear you do me wrong.

> I swear to thee, even by thine own fair eyes.

It is a society governed by law. The idea of law recurs time and again throughout the play, and it is significant that the central scene is laid in a court of law. It is part of the comic mode, too, that there should be talk of Mercy and that the youthful Portia should appear in a lawyer's gown. But the scrupulosity with which the Law should be administered and the Law's reluctance to make any exceptions are themes which also find explicit statement in the play.

In the last act the idea of order receives a subtle re-statement, and becomes the theme of exquisite poetry. External law now gives place in Lorenzo's fancy to a harmony found in immortal souls, between whom agreement is of their very essence. Music, which is a 'melody to the ear as the whole world, well understood, would afford to the understanding', induces in man and beast that sort of agreement which makes them turn their 'savage eyes' to a 'modest gaze':

> The man that hath no music in himself,
> Nor is not mov'd with concord of sweet sounds,
> Is fit for treasons, stratagems and spoils;
> The motions of his spirit are dull as night,
> And his affections dark as Erebus:
> Let no such man be trusted.

The idea of order is still order in society, but it is more deeply founded.

XVIII

Shakespeare's idea of political order has been much discussed in recent years. I shall be concerned with it only in so far as it helps me to develop the analysis of character and vision, and also in so far as it involves certain of the characters, notably Brutus, in a moral crisis which anticipates the moral crises of the great tragedies.

It is easy to reduce Shakespeare's treatment of kingship to the prose of politics, and many critics have done so. But there is one problem in Shakespeare's representation of kings which is not susceptible of this kind of treatment, for it is the indisputable work of poetry and has nothing to do with prose. This is his portrayal of royalty. Richard II is royal, even though as man he forfeits his right to be king. He is always 'royal Richard'. Henry Bolingbroke, as king, having usurped that kingdom, skilled in policy and carrying ruling authority in his mere presence, is never royal. It is Richard's tragedy that, royal as he shows himself to be, he should look for a flight of angels when he should have collected an army of men. And Bolingbroke, having no privilege as the Lord's Anointed, wins a temporal power through his command of men. And yet—such is the authority of true royalty in the vision of the play—when Richard is left without angels or men we almost feel him to have been deprived of his own. Royalty has its unmistakable style and reveals itself as certainly as greatness of soul in a work of art. It is the style in which a particular address to the world, a royal address, is transformed into poetry, and I dare say, unmistakable as it is, and absolutely unmistakable in Henry V, it defies analysis. Young Arthur has it, when he pleads with Hubert. Royalty does not exempt a man from stupidity or even from wickedness; it alone does not qualify a man to rule his kingdom. But for Shakespeare political order was something more than temporal, and was not to be explained in the handbook. There was in it a mystical element, which not prose but only poetry could represent, and a part of this element is royalty.

The histories are concerned with rebellion, usurpation, conspiracy, and war. These events are hatched in the minds of men and are exercised by the purposes of men. Certainly the idea of Fate is present in the histories, and we are continually reminded of historic expiation and retribution. But these are represented as involved with the moral nature of man, and this moral nature is apprehended in terms of its political manifestations. So it is that character is created. Shakespeare quickens the historic names with those turbulences of spirit which made them dangerous, and he represents the impact of these characters on political order. And once again the impact cannot be represented merely in terms of the prose of politics (though this is a part of the matter), nor can it be represented in terms of the psychology of the rebel. Poetry has other modes of understanding. Political order and political disorder, and those workings of man's moral nature which generate them, are all apprehended together, implying and involved with each other. Henry V is not the reconstruction of a political theorist; he is a poet's representation of a king.

Naturally, then, the studies in loyalty and in treachery

are neither simply studies in the psychological make-up of men nor simply excursions into political theory in dramatic form. In *Richard II* the Duke of York shows how difficult loyalty can be. But the difficulty does not chiefly lie in him; it lies in the nature of political order itself, shaping itself, as it must, in the authorities and the obediences of men. His dilemmas are implicit in all political purpose. Nor is it forgotten that in such a commitment there are personal as well as public obligations. At the other pole, rebellion is seen in Shakespeare's histories as a many-headed restlessness within the political order, which threatens to disrupt it, but which, at the same time, is very often a corruption and misdirection of energies which might have made that order fruitful and virtuous. We do not see proneness to rebellion simply as the headsman sees it. We see it sometimes as coming from some address to the world which, in an imperfect political order, finds only in rebellion its satisfaction and exercise. Political order is such that, while much that is evil threatens it, much that is good cannot be contained within it. And so Northumberland finds himself in the same camp with Hotspur, Hotspur with Glendower, Glendower with Worcester. All these characters are individualized with superb art in terms of Shakespeare's presiding vision of that complex of moral activities which shapes and diversifies political order.

History is more than chronicled events, and more than its abstracted economic and political causes. To make drama out of it, as Shakespeare does, is to recognize that

> Time present and time past
> Are both perhaps present in time future,

and even—for Shakespeare comes nearly to it!—that we are all members one of another. It is perhaps in the women of the play that this element in Shakespeare's vision finds most poignant representation. When they mourn a father or a husband murdered, a son in exile, or a brother solitary in some distant dungeon, they mourn—like the women of Troy, weeping amongst the fallen towers of Ilium—not for themselves alone. In them succeeding generations cry out against the act; it is their wombs which know the bitterness of loss. The Duchess of Gloucester in *Richard II* speaks not only for herself and not only of present property, but for her ancestors and her progeny and of a long heritage, when she complains that what was once a goodly home is now

> But empty lodgings and unfurnish'd walls,
> Unpeopled offices, untrodden stones.

And later in the play the Duchess of York speaks not only of her son, but of sons that might have been her son's, when she asks the Duke, who is about to denounce Aumerle:

> Have we more sons? or are we like to have?
> Is not my teeming date drunk up with time?
> And wilt thou pluck my fair son from my age,
> And rob me of a happy mother's name?

In this way the women of the histories, too, are individualized, and derive their identity, within Shakespeare's poetic vision of political order. How this order is addressed to them (but they are a part of it), what it makes of their world, how the 'pattern' is sustained in their suffering, if not in their action—all this is embodied in the women of the histories and gives them their poignant actuality.

The histories raise the problem of character-presentation in a special form. The persons in these plays, whether taken from Plutarch or Holinshed, had had already, before Shakespeare dealt with them, their particular life in men's imaginations. They were known as treacherous or ambitious; their policies had brought them victory or had come to nothing; for kings and counsellors they were famous predecessors and known examples. The audience had already formed some attitude to these characters, and, of course, this attitude was largely determined by the contemporary idea of political order. We may be sure that Shakespeare accepted these attitudes, even though he enriched and energized them. There is a sort of so-called historical play which plays tricks with such set attitudes, as in Bernard Shaw's *Caesar and Cleopatra*, and even in his *Saint Joan*. But the attitudes have to be presumed, otherwise the tricks would never come off. Shakespeare, without playing tricks, can take very good advantage of such a character: as of Hal, in his treatment of Falstaff or in the situation of Henry V's wooing, or, more movingly, in the talk with the common soldiers on the eve of Agincourt. We should remember, however, that even in these more private moments a public, a political cha-racter is being represented. It is as though a play about

Mr. Winston Churchill should show him laying bricks, giving the V sign to a crowd of women workers, and talking to the survivors of a torpedoed destroyer. Every moment is, in its own way, an image of man in political society and in these moments the character is conceived. Into the political world the study of character, however humane and individual, is extraverted.

How then is character active in the historical plays? Over all, as the presiding vision, there is a poet's idea of political order about which Shakespeare leaves us in no doubt. In *Richard II* the gardener develops the analogy between the state and the garden:

> We at time of year
> Do wound the bark, the skin of our fruit-trees,
> Lest, being over-proud in sap and blood,
> With too much richness it confound itself:
> Had he done so to great and growing men,
> They might have lived to bear and he to taste
> Their fruits of duty; superfluous branches
> We lop away, that bearing boughs may live:
> Had he done so, himself had borne the crown,
> Which waste of idle hours hath quite thrown down.

In *Henry V*, in another comparison, Shakespeare sees political society in the honey-bees, who teach 'the act of order to a peopled kingdom'. The significance of the vision expressed in these analogies in its relation to character is unmistakable. This vision, as it were, gets to know itself more concretely and more variously in such characters as Bolingbroke, Hotspur, Henry V, and Falstaff. The primary activity of character is apprehended as shaping or mis-shaping political order. And we should note that political disapproval does not imply an absolute disapproval. The bark of the tree must be wounded

> Lest, being over-proud in sap and blood,
> With too much richness it confound itself.

There is no simple opposition of sheep and goats in the internecine tensions of political society. But the political judgement, sometimes sadly enough, must override all others. I do not think that even Falstaff—setting aside his dismissal by the king—is exempt from the presiding judgement; and from that judgement he really derives his astonishing vitality. What, after all, is his speech on Honour? It is the spoken indignation of the individual in revolt against those irksome moral obligations which political order must impose. But, laugh as we may, we do not shuffle those obligations off, and we laugh because we cannot shuffle them off.

It is a consequence of all this that, in general, the characters of the historical plays have no truly private emotions. What inner feeling they may be thought to have is *public emotion*. When Henry IV complains of his sleeplessness the emotion is, as it were, a show. When Richard II takes a handful of English earth in his hands and weeps over it, the action and the feeling belong not to his private but to his public life. Even when Henry V walks round the English camp in the darkness and speaks to the common soldiers, what he says as man enlarges what he is as king.

The imagery in the historical plays has an important part in determining in what world—and in what manner—these emotions are felt. It is imagery which finds the equivalents for emotion in the world of public and political behaviour, and so this emotion takes a relevant part in our imaginative apprehension of political order.

Why, rather, sleep, liest thou in smoky cribs,
Upon uneasy pallets stretching thee,
And hush'd with buzzing night-flies to thy slumber,
Than in the perfumed chambers of the great,
Under the canopies of costly state,
And lulled with sounds of sweetest melody?

In such a way—this is a simple example—is the treatment of character subordinate to the comprehensive vision of the play, and in the presentation of character we are at all times reminded by the imagery of the political society to which character belongs.

III

THE MORAL DILEMMA IN TRAGEDY

XIX

PUBLIC decisions, nevertheless, may involve men in private moral crises. In the English histories Shakespeare, except in minor characters, as, for example, in the Duke of York in *Richard II*, does not represent his characters in moral doubt. After the event, perhaps, a character may confess the uncertainties that have attended his decisions:

> God knows, my son,
> By what by-paths and indirect crook'd ways
> I met this crown: and I myself know well
> How troublesome it sat upon my head.

But we rarely see purpose in the English histories coming to a head of decision in the will.

The Roman histories were more remote, and perhaps in *Julius Caesar* Shakespeare felt freer in his dealings with character than he did in the English histories. Besides, Plutarch gave him a different lead from the English Chronicles. In the character of Brutus, certainly, he presents the kind of moral crisis which he never treats in the English plays. The nature and significance of this crisis seem to me to have great importance in the study of Shakespeare's methods of characterization.

According to North's rendering of Plutarch, Brutus

'framed his manner of life by the rules of vertue and studie of Philosophie', and Shakespeare allows Brutus's contemporaries (and Brutus himself!) to imitate this tribute in the play. It is clear that such a character, whose constant practice it is to refer his conduct to those principles by which he directs it, will be represented with a good deal of direct self-revelation. It is also clear, however, that if these principles do in fact absolutely direct conduct, if personality is wholly contained within them, if Brutus is no more and no other than 'the noblest Roman of them all', the appeal of the play (in so far as his character is concerned) will be on a very obvious, not to say merely didactic, level. If, when Brutus says that he is 'arm'd so strong in Honesty', there is no more than that to be said, his address to the world is not at all discovered in the dramatic transformation of personality into speech and behaviour; it is discovered as an abstraction, in the reduction of personality to a set of principles. And Schücking might be held to have reason when he finds 'a certain childishness' in *Julius Caesar* which has always made the play suitable for study in schools.

Before we agree with Schücking we should look at the matter a little more closely. Thus Mr. J. I. M. Stewart, in the book already cited, suggests that the play (and the study of the character of Brutus) has in it 'more subtlety than is readily discernible'. He applies to Brutus's reiterated claims to unusual honesty a psychological interpretation, and he holds that these claims show Brutus's motives to have been more selfish than he himself suspected. He believes that Brutus, with some intellectual dishonesty, uses a form of self-deception to 'cheer himself up'. Brutus, Mr. J. I. M. Stewart suggests, keeps insisting to himself that he is honest in order to keep out of his consciousness the wrinkling doubts.

This interpretation, which is little more than a sophisticating application of the maxim *Qui s'excuse s'accuse*, will surely never do. There is another explanation in which not only Shakespeare's subtlety but also an important, perhaps the most important, element in his treatment of the tragic character is more easily discernible. The issue is not psychological but moral. Brutus is honest, intellectually and all-otherwise. So far as conduct in this life can be guided by principles, his is so guided. And yet it must certainly be thought that the decision on the ground of these principles to kill Caesar was not easily or speedily arrived at, and there is no reason to suppose (and no evidence) that a certain 'fumbling' in the decisive soliloquy in any way implies a specific impurity of motive. A man may be sure of his principles and doubtful of their exercise. This 'fumbling', this uncertainty, is premonitory evidence of the moral issue of the play, so far as Brutus is concerned in it; that the moral decision must be made, but that even in the making of it and whatever the decision may be, Brutus will be involved in moral error. This error is no specific impurity, such as unlawful or even unconscious ambition; it is an error inherent in the decision itself, in all decisions, even in their 'honesty'. There could perhaps be no more significant comment on the relation between the private moral judgement and the apprehension of all political order whatsoever. It is a terrible thought but a true one: the statesman is never right, but to choose the right he must continually endeavour. And this is true of every man, in all moral activity.

It must not be thought, however, that succeeding external events only prove him wrong—the fickleness of the Roman mob, the extortion of money by Cassius, imminent defeat—they merely suggest the bewildering truth, but it is a truth not dependent on temporal occasions. External events cast an ironical shadow over the honesty of Brutus, and we marvel that in such good could be mixed such evil. As Brutus's fortunes decline our moral vision grows more widely comprehending, but it is no argument from failure that makes us question the earlier decision. It is not merely failure that deepens that vision with the recognition that attachment to honesty may be attachment to my honesty, and that it is not only Brutus's honesty that is impugned but all mortal honesty whatsoever. To find the flaw in this honesty in something particular to the act, making it dishonest, is to destroy the meaning of the play. For the study of Brutus is a study in that evil original in our flesh which brings in a little corruption—and often more than a little—whenever man, in decision and action, addresses himself, as he must, to his world.

xx

In *Hamlet* Shakespeare attempts the most comprehensive study of precisely the same moral problem. It may be true that a man will hesitate if there is in him 'a pre-valence of the abstracting and generalizing habit over the practical', or if he indulges in a 'great, an almost enormous intellectual activity, and a proportionate aversion to real action'. It may be true that a man will refrain from an action which will release into the day-light those terrible impulses which had hitherto lain hidden in the darkness of the unconscious. It may even be true that to kill a king is no simple matter and that certain arrangements must be made before it can be effected. Coleridge, Jones, and Stoll all offer plausible reasons why Hamlet delayed. But to Coleridge, we must answer—Yes, but that is to say no more than that Hamlet delayed; and to Jones—Perhaps, but that is not what the play is about; and to Stoll—Laertes made short and sharp arrangements to kill a prince.

Hamlet, despite all explanations, remains a puzzle—because it is a puzzle. It defies explanation because there is no explanation—at least, so long as an explanation is sought in the character of Hamlet himself. For this character is Shakespeare's most fundamental, most uni-versal study—I do not say a wholly satisfactory study—of the moral nature of man's address to his world. *Hamlet* is not a challenge to our psychological ingenuity; it is a challenge to the faith we seek to live by. The puzzle and the explanation both lie in our common predicament; that action is imperative for man, but that all action whatsoever involves man in evil. I do not say that Shakespeare is explicitly aware of this; or that he projects any such awareness into the mind of Hamlet as he represents it. Nevertheless, it seems to me to be the only way in which we can explain the universality of the Hamlet-theme, and the way in which that universality has defied elaboration.

I do not see how otherwise to interpret the 'To be or not to be' soliloquy, for this is certainly a soliloquy in which Shakespeare makes a set consideration of man's address to his world. There are two themes in the soliloquy, one latent, the other explicit. The explicit theme is the theme of suicide. Would not a man 'his quietus make with a bare bodkin' but for the 'dread of something after death'? But to commit suicide is to cancel moral responsibility—or so it would be, one might think, but for this 'dread'. Perhaps—so the thought runs—to die is not to cancel this responsibility; perhaps, even after death, responsibility persists. The latent theme follows from this and is involved in it. It is the theme of man in dilemma between action and inaction:

> Whether 'tis nobler in the mind to suffer
> The slings and arrows of outrageous fortune,
> Or to take arms against a sea of troubles,
> And, by opposing, end them?

And at the end of the soliloquy the explicit sense of what has gone before is not sufficient to explain Hamlet's thoughts; the latent sense almost presides over the thinking:

> And thus the native hue of resolution
> Is sicklied o'er with the pale cast of thought;

And enterprises of great pith and moment,
With this regard, their currents turn awry,
And lose the name of action.

The same theme, latent here, almost comes into the
light of day in a later soliloquy:

What is a man,
If his chief good and market of his time
Be but to sleep and feed? a beast, no more.
Sure he that hath made us with such large discourse,
Looking before and after, gave us not
That capability and god-like reason
To fust in us unus'd.

Reason is moral reason, which looks before and after.
Hamlet here is persuading himself that, whatever evil
and whatever death may be the consequence of action,
man's reason is god-like and should not grow stale
through lack of use. To address ourselves to the world in
action may involve us in evil; but not so to address ourselves is to be less than man.

It is part of the irony of the play, and perhaps some
reason for supposing it in some degree an 'artistic
failure', that whenever Hamlet for a moment contem-
plates action and whenever he acts, the 'god-like reason'
seems to have little to do with it. But to consider this
aspect of the matter is not within my purpose. My purpose is to illustrate from *Hamlet* that the play is not the
study of a man, but the study of the moral nature of a
man in his traffic with the outer world; to suggest that
character and moral vision must be apprehended together, and that when character is understood separately
from moral vision it is not in fact understood at all.

XXI

It is equally true to say that moral vision must not be understood apart from character, since character is moral vision getting to know itself.

When I come to write about the great tragedies and the 'Romances' I shall have occasion to suggest that the Christian-allegorical interpretations recently placed upon certain of Shakespeare's works (especially *King Lear* and *The Winter's Tale*) are almost certainly in error. At this point I want to discuss a specific instance in which this allegorical interpretation has been argued (or, at least, illustrated) from a mistaken view of a particular character—a mistaken view, indeed, of the treatment of character in general. In his book *Shakespeare's Doctrine of Nature* Mr. John F. Danby supports his Christian interpretation of the play with an analysis of the character of Cordelia. He writes:

> In our view, she is a figure comparable with that of Griselde or Beatrice: literally a woman: allegorically the root of individual and social sanity; tropologically charity 'that suffereth long and is kind'; anagogically the redemptive principle itself. . . .

Much depends, as Mr. Danby recognizes, on our interpretation of Cordelia's conduct—and character—in the First Act, and on Mr. Danby's defence of Cordelia against the accusation of 'pride'. He appeals to common sense to distinguish between 'the virtue that feeds a sense of pride' and 'the proper obdurateness of virtue standing its ground against hypocrisy and wrong-

headedness'. Cordelia, he claims, bases her behaviour
'in simple truth' on a system of rightness in human relations. Cordelia loves the king, according to her 'bond'—
neither less nor more. And the word 'bond' has a double
meaning; it means 'natural tie' and it means 'obligation', the one being a way of looking at the other. What
self-regarding impulse there is in her behaviour is no
more than that proper love of self which is the beginning of the love of God and of one's neighbour.

This seems to me greatly to over-simplify the moral
significance of the scene. Is not Cordelia's conduct—
even though, morally, she could do no other—the kind
of conduct for which she must go down on her knees and
ask forgiveness? She must ask forgiveness, surely, for
repeating that word 'Nothing' when Lear bids her
speak; for this is not the 'simple truth'. She must ask
forgiveness (even on the basis of Mr. Danby's annota-
tion) for using the word 'bond' in an equivocal sense,
for she intends, or at least must know, that the one
sense and not the other will strike a chill in the old
man's heart. And this need for forgiveness is made clear
for us in the text in a passage which Mr. Danby does
not, in this connexion, quote. Almost immediately
Cordelia is put to it to justify herself, and what is self-
justification but the attempt to restore, after loss, the
'proper love of oneself', an admission of the need for
forgiveness?

> I yet beseech your Majesty—
> If for I want that glib and oily art
> To speak and purpose not—

(Is there not a hint of 'pride' in this?)

>   —since what I well contend,
> I'll do it before I speak—that you make known
> It is no vicious blot nor other foulness,
> No unchaste action, or dishonour'd step
> That hath deprived me of your grace and favour;
> But even for want of that for which I am richer,
> A still-soliciting eye, and such a tongue
> That I am glad I have not, though not to have it
> Hath lost me in your liking.

She must ask forgiveness, surely, for taking out on an old man, however silly his game might have been, her disgust with her sisters. And—this is the crux of the matter—whatever she did, she would have had to ask forgiveness. Human relations are indeed, as Mr. Danby suggests, such that men must make for themselves a 'system of rightness'; but in applying that system men run the danger of poisoning those very relations which they seek to organize.

In an 'anagogical sense', Mr. Danby believes that Cordelia is the 'redemptive principle itself'. He supports this by what seems to be a plausible but not certain reading of the lines in Act IV, scene vi, when the gentleman says of Cordelia:

>   Thou hast one daughter
> Who redeems Nature from the general curse
> Which twain have brought her to.

It is hard to believe that Shakespeare should introduce so casually and so cryptically his most direct evidence that Cordelia has to do with 'the supernal things of eternal glory'. If Mr. Danby is in error, as I think he is, in his interpretation of Cordelia's conduct in the first Act, it must be supposed that we have in these lines no more than bold and moving allusion to those 'things'. Not in this way, indeed, can the 'literal' representation of a character be brought together with the 'anagogical'. If we think of the character of Cordelia as vision in the process of getting to know itself, we can hardly accept the Christian interpretation as Mr. Danby outlines it; for this character, so much more humanly moving than he supposes, in no way sustains the allegorical function which he assigns to it.

XXII

The idea that any act of the will necessarily involves us in evil has had various histories in Western and Eastern philosophy. In one form or another, however, it is part of the 'perennial philosophy', and it is, perhaps, at the root of all great tragedy. Certainly it is implicit in Sophoclean irony. There is a sense in which any act of the will may be regarded as an effort at self-transcendence; and there is a sense, too, in which any act of the will is an act of self-attachment. The Christian view affirms that self-transcendence and self-attachment (the 'proper love of oneself') can only be reconciled by grace, in those wills which have become 'ingrafted in Christ'. It is an element, at least, in the tragic view of life that man 'never is but always to be blest'.

IV

CHANGE IN THE TRAGIC CHARACTER

XXIII

THERE is a general agreement that in Shakespeare's tragedies we witness a process of 'chemical change' in the hero's spirit, brought about by a situation which makes demands upon him which he cannot fulfil and by a moral failure which has its issue at last in a reorganization of his whole being. Character-change and character-development, at any rate, are fundamental elements in Shakespeare's great tragic dramas. He was not only concerned with what happens to a man; he was also concerned with what happens within a man. The nature of this change and development is crucial in an understanding of the relation between Shakespeare's vision and his creation of the tragic characters.

Before I discuss that, however, it seems to me useful to consider the nature of 'change' in certain other characters created in another mode.

In *The Winter's Tale* and *The Tempest* the characters of Leontes, Alonzo, and Sebastian undergo what certainly appears to be character-development, going hand in hand with repentance and reconciliation at the end of the play. Leontes, having learned the truth, repents immediately, but has to wait sixteen years for reconciliation. Alonzo and Sebastian are taught a brief but bitter lesson by Prospero. We would say, in everyday language, that they become changed men, and it is part of the optimism of tragi-comic effect that we should suppose the change to be lasting. The motivation of the change, and the evidence for its probable permanence, do not seem to be wholly adequate and are, at least, mainly mechanical. How mechanical it is we may illustrate perhaps from the extreme case of Iachimo. The inner transformation (if we suppose there to be one) is only conveniently brought about: in Leontes by the words of the oracle declaring Hermione to be chaste, and in Alonzo and Sebastian by the discomforts and distresses which Prospero imposes upon them. Attitude before and attitude after are really opaque to each other, although they are credibly represented as belonging to the one character. Personality is not reorganized but metamorphosed. We recognize the new address to life, the change in mental attitude, but Shakespeare has been little concerned (Alonzo and Sebastian are, of course, minor characters) to explore and justify those deeper processes by which this change might have been brought about.

Why, then, are we convinced by the change—or, at least, why do we accept it?

For two reasons, I think. In the first place, these characters change in a manner directly and unambiguously derived from the comprehensive (and ultimately optimistic) vision of the play. In the play's magnetic field, as it were, we do not doubt that all the characters will be drawn towards the pole. Just as character itself may be directly determined by the moral vision of the play, so also in the same way what happens to character and within character may be so determined and made credible. Secondly, the change in character is one which we approve and which agrees with the social judgement. It is a return to what is more desirable by way of nature; for in the Romances evil in man is an accident and not the original condition of his being. Repentance and forgiveness, after all, conserve order and harmony in society. Such changes need no deeper motivation than the persuasion of external events. If a man is punished, we grant that he will do better in future. If a man is undeceived, we grant that he will not persist in folly. It is the assumption of comedy that men and women are capable of being educated, and in comedy the Law (as it were) is often a schoolmaster to bring men to their senses. At least, as with Lucio in *Measure for Measure*, they can be restrained. We do not, then, in characters such as these discover any real change. We discover rather a change of attitude, the result not of any inner motivation but of the teaching of external events. In something the same way, we might say, Elizabeth Bennet loses her prejudice, and Darcy forgets his pride; marriage (we believe) will see to it that there is no backsliding. What the readers, what the audience, *want* to believe, determines what is, in fact, credible.

XXIV

Even more illuminating than the treatment of the characters just mentioned from the Romances is the treatment of the character of Angelo in *Measure for Measure*. He, too, undergoes changes, and changes of a very dramatic kind; and he has always been something of a puzzle to the critics. It is possible that the groundlings saw Angelo as a mere hypocrite, who sent them back to their viciousness with the comfortable feeling that the seeming best of men have the itch as much as they. But it is quite clear that Shakespeare intended something more serious than that. It is also possible to see in Angelo the study of a man whose appetites have been too tightly reined, and who is overwhelmed by a 'fetichistic' lust for a girl who comes in the robes of the nunnery to plead for her brother's life. And we can begin with this view in our attempt to relate the study of Angelo to the general vision of the play. For Angelo must be what the vision of the play makes of him. If, for example, the play is, as R. W. Chambers suggested, a study in penitence and punishment, and if it ends with the 'stuff of Christianity', the idea of redemption, then the psychological study of this 'fetichistic lust' must be auxiliary to a study of the moral nature of man. If Angelo is to be seen in the end as fallen man redeemed, Shakespeare's study of him must be the study of a human soul.

One preliminary comment is necessary. What may be held (if anything at all) to be unsatisfactory or incomplete in the study of Angelo has been explained and excused by the fact that he is by no means the central figure of the play, and consequently a certain morbidity may be allowed in his character—as though what is morbid, though shading into the 'normal', may properly be part of the periphery of attention. One may suppose, that is to say, that a pathological study, when it is not the heart and centre of the play, may nevertheless be properly introduced into the play, since the moral has to do with the pathological, and who shall say where the one becomes the other? Angelo's case, had it been the centre of the play, would have been morbid, because it is not universal. Since it is not the centre, so the argument runs, it serves to darken and deepen the universality of the play, and has, as it were by derivation, a secondary, a derived universality.

If this is so, however, criticism must not load the morbidity with more significance than it can bear. It must not say: The play is about 'redemption', therefore Angelo is redeemed, *and* therefore his conduct can only have such-and-such an interpretation. Criticism, having decided that the theme of the play is a study in 'penitence and punishment', must not read into the character a psychological subtlety and a moral understanding which could only have been there if that character had been a central character in the play. Criticism must not proceed on the lines of the hypothesis—Now what should I have had to say of this character had he been the central character of the play? And this is precisely what Mr. J. I. M. Stewart, in his concern to defend Shakespeare against Dr. Bridges, does when he writes: 'In the last act of the play [Angelo] is like a man fighting his way through a dream, loaded with the awful consciousness of having done irreparable ill.' This judgement might apply to Macbeth, but not to Angelo. For the last act of the play in no way bears this out, as I shall shortly have occasion to show. The truth is that such words as Mr. Stewart uses ought only to be used about a central character whose 'awful consciousness' has indeed been the central study of the play.

We learn enough about Angelo, even though he is not the central character, to know that he is involved in the most awful moral crisis of the play; a moral crisis in which might well have been represented the universal crisis of man, in which there might have been a particular exposure of man's fall from grace. Indeed, the main responsibility for representing this case of man is laid on Angelo; but Angelo cannot properly represent it, just because he is not the central character of the play.

Nor is it at all the concern of *Measure for Measure* to make such a study of 'awful consciousness'. The world of the play is not really the world of human souls. It is true that in the last act there is some play with the notions of penitence and forgiveness; the Law is threatened and then remitted. But the play is called *Measure for Measure*, and the deeper seriousness of penitence and forgiveness are uneasily accommodated in the treatment of such a theme. The final concern of the play is not with redemption or with grace but with the Law, and when the Law seems at the end of the play to be abrogated it is surely an error to suppose that its place has been taken by a covenant of grace. For the Law, in fact, is not abrogated. The marriages imposed—Angelo's as much as Lucio's—are salutary, not blessed. This so-called forgiveness, this remission of the Law, is in some ways more terrible than the rigour of the law suspended; for it implies that lust may, after all, be bridled as well by marriage as by death. Angelo's marriage is not very different from Lucio's; it is not, surely, the marriage of a man who has undergone a 'saving experience'. It is a marriage which will conserve (and perhaps continuate) the society to which both Angelo and Lucio belong.

No world of evil makes a bid in *Measure for Measure* for the soul of a man, for such a world always both is and is not the creation of man. The lust that overwhelms Angelo seems to spring, psychologically, from within, but in a truer sense it overwhelms him from without. It does not come to him as a revelation of himself, as Macbeth's ambitious purpose both surprises and convicts him and makes him tremble as at a revelation of himself. There is always a separateness between Angelo and his lust; and the lust is simple and opaque, except after psychological analysis, to the earlier nature of the man. Angelo's lust has no more poetry in it than rape in a court of law; and had he indeed belonged to the world of human souls the lust would have been pitifully, terribly, in the poetry. And so in Angelo, changed and remorseful, what was this lust, never having been other than separate from him, can only be destroyed. In a human soul all may be transformed, but nothing destroyed.

Nevertheless, the implied agony and the moral seriousness of Angelo's case are such that they cannot be sustained unless he is seen—unless in Shakespeare's vision he has been apprehended—as a human soul. For we refuse to accept him either as a study in morbid psychology or as a canting hypocrite. We must conclude, then, that in Angelo Shakespeare has introduced a situation, a case, and a character, intractable to the working out of the comprehensive vision of the play. And this is as much as to say that the vision itself is uncertain, for vision seeks to discover itself in character.

In Angelo, vision does not so discover itself, and it is instructive to note in what manner and measure it fails. The imagery in which Angelo expresses himself scarcely ever reveals the darker recesses of his being; nothing rises from the centre. The promptings of his lust express themselves in external figures, in the very language of the Law, and the appetite has no status or activity in the world of the spirit. Once recognized, it turns outward to explain itself, using language which takes its substance and its currency from secular society.

> O heavens!
> Why does my blood thus muster to my heart,
> Making both it unable for itself,
> And dispossessing all my other parts
> Of necessary fitness?

Then, immediately, Angelo turns to a mere simile, a memory from social experience, elaborating but not enriching, not generating the emotion:

> So play the foolish throngs with one that swounds;
> Come all to help him, and so stop the air
> At which he would revive.

This is not the appetite speaking, but the man about the appetite. So, later, lust takes its language from the Law, and loses thereby its nature, since it takes this language and leaves it untransformed. It speaks of 'accusation', 'calumnies', 'seeing', 'banishment', and 'lingering sufferance'. Even after the satisfaction, Angelo does not see the evil he has done except in these terms of Law and reputation—and some doubts about his own safety:

> This deed unshapes me quite, makes me unpregnant
> And dull to all proceedings. A deflower'd maid,
> And by an eminent body that enforc'd
> The Law against it! But that her tender shame
> Will not proclaim against her maiden loss,
> How might she tongue me! Yet reason dares her no;
> For my authority bears so credent bulk,
> That no particular scandal once can touch;
> But it confounds the breather.

There is no penitence here; there is no exhaustion of lustful appetite; the lawyer is talking about the lecher. It is not for nothing that at the end of the last Act the Duke says, when Claudio is known to be still alive:

> By this, Lord Angelo perceives he's safe:
> Methinks I see a quickening in his eye.

The Duke speaks here of a man not redeemed but reprieved. But there is something in Angelo's case, and in the treatment of that case, which would make us wish him both redeemed and reprieved.

XXV

I have spoken throughout this essay of vision, discovering itself in character and in conflict between characters, as though vision itself was unfolded in the play, and as though this unfolding was achieved through the embodiment in characters of various addresses to life, all presided over by one supreme and comprehensive address, which was Shakespeare's. The vision discovered, though complex and organic, is seen to be static; and that it is so may be shown by the fact that there is no example in the comedies or the histories of deep change in character, or, at least, there is no change which cannot be accommodated to the social and moral judgements implicit in the play. Speaking generally, we may say that in the comedies and the histories vision is generated and deepened, but not transformed. As we read the play we undergo an illuminating but not a changing experience; and when we put it down we understand better, but not differently. Here, I fancy, is the clue to that representation of the human soul which is the business of the great tragedies; the process by which vision discovers itself in character is a process of catharsis, and the purification that leaves the hero serene for death is at one with the purification which we ourselves must know. In the tragedies, character not only discovers, it also transforms vision; we have not only creation, but transfiguration.

In the comedies, where the social sense was lightly but assuredly—and not so lightly in the so-called 'dark' comedies—affirmed, the Comic Muse was regulative. It corrected with a smile, with a touch of irony, and (as in *Twelfth Night*) with a little melancholy, the modest assaults made on social order and social decorum. After all, there was no danger of the world ever being peopled by Gobbos or even by Jews; and, once married, the Duke no longer sighs in Illyria. The storms that drive Antonio's argosies from their course make only a temporary distemper in that general favour of the Mediterranean which will shortly bring them home.

In the histories, even where disorder most threatens, we have a sure expectation that it will not triumph, and the order that will shortly be established always presides over our attitudes and hopes. The ideal of political order remains constant in the histories, and in terms of that ideal vision and character are formed. Vision remains itself and character undergoes no transforming change. Our attitudes are never at a loss, and when Henry V comes into his kingdom we know that at last we are where we had hoped to be.

In the comedies and the histories there is never any real doubt about the world-picture into which the characters must be fitted, and in terms of which the characters find identity. And in so far as this world-picture involves also a world beyond this world, it may be said that that other world is the Christian universe; but Shakespeare's concern in these plays is secular and social, and his vision scarcely comprehends the play of forces beyond the stage of Time. It is not in terms of the play of such metaphysical forces that character must be apprehended. There is little in the comedies that the Comic Muse cannot deal with: in the histories there is little that the Prince cannot take into account.

In the great tragedies, however, just as there is change and development within the character, so also is there change and development within the vision of the play. So far as character is concerned, the pattern of the tragedies has often been remarked upon. The hero is confronted by a situation with which the organization of his being is unable to cope. He loses his moral bearings; he is at a loss; his whole personality seems to disintegrate more and more wilfully towards destruction. In the end, chastened and changed, he is absolute for death. But there is also a parallel, perhaps an underlying, development of vision accompanying this process in character. This development reveals itself in a change in our attitudes, although it concerns something more than attitude. We have already seen how in the Romances character can seem to change without involving a change of vision; and we have also seen how in the comedies something can happen to a character (as with Shylock, Malvolio, and, perhaps, with Falstaff) which asks from us a change in attitude which we cannot very well make. In the tragedies the hero undergoes an experience which puts all our previous attitude into question and which exacts from us, as from him, a transformation of vision which can accommodate and appropriate the new and uncovenanted experience.

XXVI

If the tragic heroes could be apprehended in terms of the temporal and secular world, social and political judgements would be adequate to deal with them. The great Shakespearian tragedies, however, are what they are just because social and political judgements (though never wholly abrogated) tend to break down. Consequently we must say of Hamlet, Macbeth, Othello, and King Lear that in some part of their natures they belong not to the temporal world but to a world beyond the world, a universe outside time, and that in this way we must apprehend them. In other words, vision, fulfilling itself in these characters, is no longer contained within society, legal, moral, or political, but seeks, as it were, to transcend society, to judge the social judgement, to bring society and its judgements *sub specie aeternitatis*. So—Macbeth is a villain; but when Duncan lies dead in the next room we think not of the murder but of the horror of Macbeth's realization that he shall sleep no more. He is for the moment like a soul in hell, and this is hell, nor is he out of it, and we know a little more about hell because Macbeth has had a glimpse of it. These tragedies, then, all imply a metaphysical world in which what matters is not what men do to society but what they do to themselves. This is the major vision which seeks to fulfil itself in the tragic heroes. It is only, perhaps, in *King Lear* that this vision so enlarges itself that it almost comprehends the supreme truth that what men do to themselves cannot, even in thought, be separated from what men do to society, and that the love of one's neighbour is the proper love of oneself. This theme, however, I reserve for a future section.

The great tragic heroes are the only characters who address themselves to a metaphysical world in such a way that we feel them to be citizens of that world as much as of this. Their special contact with that world is variously represented, and with varying emphasis; perhaps the citizenship only becomes absolute in *Macbeth*, but in some measure all are endowed with it.

In *Hamlet*, although Horatio and Marcellus first see the ghost, only Hamlet is spoken to and only Hamlet is made privy to the ghost's purposes. But Hamlet's citizenship in the metaphysical world is not only suggested by his traffic with the ghost; it is also brought home to us by all those speculations on death and what comes after death. Hamlet speaks in images which come from man's solitary experiences as well as from his experiences of social and political society—from the intuitions, troubled certitudes, in which we become aware of this world as islanded, indeed, though in a sea of doubt. In *Hamlet*, certainly, we can say that vision is seeking, perhaps self-consciously, to settle the human soul in its relation with an everlasting universe. And we can see this just as clearly when Hamlet holds Yorick's skull in his hand as when he wonders 'To be or not to be'. The settlement is never ratified, but at least we come to the serenity of 'The readiness is all'.

Othello habitually assumes his membership of a universe, beyond and often invisible to this, and he

seems to come amongst the Venetians with an authority
and an identity derived elsewhere.

> And when I love thee not
> Chaos is come again.

> Methinks it should be now a huge eclipse
> Of sun and moon, and that the affrighted globe
> Should yawn at alteration.

Othello's mind (excellent general though he was) never
expresses itself in secular terms. The invisible universe
is all about him; the sun, the moon, and the oceans are
the hiding-places of spiritual energies, the analogies
of spiritual power. Othello has no need of ghosts or
supernatural beings to prove his acquaintance with
this universe. His distinction amongst men is this—
that he treads the earth with all the authority of a
man who belongs elsewhere. He is, by contrast with
the others, apprehended by us as a religious man, a
human soul.

Macbeth delivers himself absolutely to a darker
world. He is exiled from the daylight. It is not only that
he is familiar with the witches and that the ghost of
Banquo appears only to him; his imagination draws on
assurances and presences which do not come to him from
temporal experience, and his discovery of this world of
darkness has the authority of a revelation.

I have already suggested that in *Lear* the matter
is a little different. Nevertheless, Lear is certainly
elemented with the thunder and the wind, with the
heavens themselves, and he thinks it no arrogance to
reproach the gods. But he is also more than the other

tragic characters the creature of secular society. In so far as he belongs to the invisible universe, however, he reveals an original and primitive kinship in man with things and beings in a state of Nature, with the natural universe itself. When on the moor he seems to cancel for the time being all temporal affiliations, yet presently he remembers the 'poor naked wretches' of the world. He belongs, indeed, to the world of Nature (and this in a metaphysical sense), but only because, as we shall see, he is the central character in a play which takes as its theme the fulfilment of Nature in human Society. In the other tragedies, this world and the metaphysical world are in one way or another discontinuous; in *Lear* they are perceived as one, and in some measure not only Lear himself but all the other characters belong to both.

XXVII

Does Antony belong to such a world? Or Coriolanus? If we consider the matter attentively, we shall perceive that these two characters are wholly expressed within time, and are contained within the social judgement. There is no mystery about them. Theirs is the world of Rome and Egypt, and what traffic they have is with Romans, Egyptians, and Volscians. Even though Antony uses hyperbole as extravagant as Othello's, the effect is quite different.

> Let Rome in Tiber melt . . .

> Alack! our terrene moon
> Is now eclipsed; and it portends alone
> The fall of Antony.

But in these images Antony is aggrandized; he is not translated. Language matches his magnificence, but it leaves the order of magnificence unchanged. Antony may evoke the sun, the moon, and the stars; Othello addresses himself to that universe of which they and he are constituent elements. In Antony such images are a manner of speaking; in Othello, they are his way of apprehending the very processes of the universe. Through Antony vision does not seek to know something of the metaphysical universe, and Antony himself is in no way a religious man. Something of all this, too, must be said of Coriolanus, and of Timon. These are none of them men for whose souls there is competition between the forces of good and the forces of evil.

XXVIII

An important corollary of this view of the tragic hero concerns the attitude of the audience. Attitude in an audience tends to be social attitude. Social attitude, however, is irrelevant, or only partly relevant, in the creation of the tragic hero. From one point of view he seems to claim exemption from the social and moral judgement. If this were not so, we might agree forthwith with Thomas Rymer and have done with the matter. But if he claims this exemption and receives it, he is thereby distinguished from the characters in the comedies and the histories, who are what they are at least partly because of the social attitude generated towards them and the social judgement made on them. The tragic heroes, then, do not address themselves to the audience in the same way as these other characters.

We have seen, earlier in this essay, that many of the earlier characters, perhaps most of them, establish a *rapport* with the audience not unlike that established by the comedian in the music-hall. And it is quite certain that even in the tragedies a character such as Iago must establish that same kind of *rapport*. But you cannot say of the tragic character as you can say of these—that without an audience they have no identity. An audience is necessary, one would think, to those characters who are viewed *sub specie temporis*; but the tragic character is also viewed *sub specie aeternitatis*.

It is the distinction of the tragic character that we have some idea what he is in his solitudes. In this he differs from the comic and the historical characters, who are never alone, who are always either in the company of other characters or in the presence of the audience, and who at all times present themselves either to the other characters or to the audience, The eyes of the present world are always on these characters, and it is as if they knew it. It is significant that after the great tragedies, in *Antony and Cleopatra*, in *Coriolanus*, and (*per contra*) in *Timon*, Shakespeare's major theme once again becomes the eyes of the present world, 'the world's report', as though he were consciously taking up again the secular vision which he had for so long abandoned. For his interest in what the tragic hero is in his solitude is not a secular but a religious interest; since a man's religion is at least partly what he does with his solitude.

And in the tragic characters Shakespeare's concern, and ours, is to look through their eyes, when they are alone, and to seek with them, through failure and disaster, to make such terms as we can with the metaphysical universe. To do this Shakespeare had to effect a significant balance between the sense of actuality which we find in a character when it establishes *rapport* with the audience and that exemption from the social judgement which may be granted to characters with whom in part we seek to identify ourselves. For in the tragic characters it is certainly true that Shakespeare 'darts himself forth', however much it is also true that he remains himself at the same time. And it is true of us, also; but the identification is moral, not psychological.

XXIX

The tragic situation in an elementary form is to be found in the discomfitures that attend Shylock, Malvolio, and perhaps Falstaff. Each of these characters is faced by or brought to a situation for which his previous address to the world had never covenanted. To meet this situation that address must be transformed, and it must be transformed from within. They are thrown on resources within themselves and they are, for the time, alone. Hatred, wit, self-love have lost their outside sources of sustenance. They no longer serve. In addition, however, there has been induced in us an attitude to the character which is as much at a loss in the new situation as the character's own address to life. We, too, had never covenanted for this moment, and whereas, before, these characters had largely drawn their identity from our attitudes to them, we are suddenly called upon to share with them, in sympathy, their attitude to life. Only by becoming one with Shylock can we know what Shylock must do now; and so it is with Falstaff and Malvolio. For the manner in which we have hitherto regarded these characters has become irrelevant. The social attitude is asked to give way to something to which we can scarcely give a name, 'without it be compassion'. The social attitude, however, does not so easily accommodate itself, and we can give to these persons in their misfortune little more than that less significant pity which we give to unlucky people in real life. In the tragedies just as the hero's attitude to life proves inadequate and is transformed, so our attitude to the hero proves irrelevant and is transformed. And these two transformations work in him—and, through him, in us—an enrichment, a transformation of vision. True compassion, after all, is a religious emotion.

The change in the tragic hero is, then, not only and not chiefly a psychological change; it is a moral change, a conversion, a change in vision. It is a total resettlement of his moral being. But it is more than that, for in it vision seems to transform for us the universe itself. So in the scene on the heath, before the hovel, when Lear remembers the 'poor naked wretches'—

> Poor naked wretches, wheresoe'er you are
> That bide the pelting of the pitiless storm,
> How shall your houseless heads, and unfed sides,

Your loop'd and window'd raggedness, defend you
From seasons such as these?

Lear is revealing not only personality in a process of
change but a mind making a discovery for itself and
about itself, and being transformed in the process. For
Lear the world is, indeed, a 'vale of soul-making'. And
the making of a soul is the transformation of man's universe as well as of man himself—

Oh! I have ta'en
Too little care of this. Take physic, pomp;
Expose thyself to feel what wretches feel,
That thou may'st shake the superflux to them,
And show the heavens more just.

The vision of the world—one might say the world itself,
in so far as it is a moral world—in which personality has
its being is itself reordered and refashioned. Not only
man but the heavens themselves will seem 'more just'.
To apprehend the character is to apprehend much more
than character. Lear's madness gives us a glimpse of
Chaos; and it gives us the hope, too, that out of such
Chaos, as by a transubstantiation, Blessedness is somehow born.

XXX

We impoverish poetic drama if we suppose that the
creation of a character such as Lear is no more than the
'study of a man'. When Lear thinks of the 'poor naked
wretches' we know for a moment something of the process of redemption; but, what is more, the universe is,
for that moment, saved from hatred and frenzy for

sanity and pity. When Lear bids 'copulation thrive' and sees all civil state in rank perversion we know something for a moment of the soul's abandonment; but, what is more, we fear the delivery of the universe to foul disorder. Of course our concern is with a man, with Lear; but our concern with him is this—the manner in which, even in his madness, he addresses himself to the universe and the manner in which, in that address, the universe is seen anew.

To bring to bear the findings of psychopathology on the study of Lear is, in fact, not to make a study of a man. For what particularity is there in the dog-fish we dissect in the laboratory? The dissection is a waste of time unless we assume that one dog-fish is like any other dog-fish, similarly whole or similarly diseased. What do we do with Lear when we psychoanalyse his madness? We reduce him to the shabby validity of our generalizations. Lear's conduct, however, is not properly subject to these generalizations, for this conduct belongs not to the realm of motivation but to the realm of volition, of moral responsibilities. Lear's individuality is moral, not psychological, and his breakdown likewise is moral rather than mental. The world to which Lear belongs is a world beyond the scrutiny of the psychologist—it is, in its ideal form, a kingdom of ends; and it is in the light of this ideal form that Lear is known and realized as a human soul.

Poetry is the language of this kingdom, and it is in poetry that vision fulfils itself in the tragic character. Images drawn from the dark resources of our minds, from the unconditioned places of our being, do not come to us in poetic drama, rich primarily in those ambiguities which guide the diagnosis of the clinical psychologist. They come rather as dark materials out of which the character, and through him Shakespeare, frames a new settlement of his spirit, a new order in his vision of the world. They are the materials of his moral being, his moral vision. The tragic characters are, indeed, called upon to do what no other character is called upon to do—to refashion themselves, to reframe their universe, out of Chaos; and this they do in the poetry.

XXXI

What is done in the poetry is done at least partly through the imagery; and the relation between character and vision in the tragedies can best be discovered in the nature of the imagery. For our interest in the character is very largely our interest in what the character makes of his universe, and what the character makes of his universe is very largely what is wrought in the imagery. And the imagery reflects the fact that both vision and character in the major tragedies are dynamic, and not, as in the comedies, static.

There is a distinction between kinds of images which has not, I believe, received the attention it merits. The content of an image—its associations and reverberations —may be derived either from experience settled and ordered in society or from experience unconditioned and private from our solitudes. Imagery may affirm a public world, or suggest and create a private world. It must be observed, too, that the same image may come to us at different times with different associations. An image is what it is at least partly because of its context, and thence it derives its peculiar activity. The activity of these different kinds of image varies, too; for a preponderance of the first kind, as in the *Merchant of Venice*, will reinforce our assurance of social and public order; but a preponderance of the second will demand from us a continual and dynamic settlement after unsettlement, the fashioning of a new order within disorder. This latter is the experience we share with the tragic hero and it is the process by which vision is discovered and transformed in the great tragedies. In the comedies and the histories the imagery presents us with a world and a society already ideally ordered; in the tragedies the imagery is such that it demands from us (as it does from the hero) a return, as it were, to the origins of order, and, from these origins, and within the poetic activity, it prompts in us the shaping and fashioning of order quite anew.

It is for this reason that when we listen to Iago we have the impression that no more is going on inside him than is explicit in what he says; but in Othello from moment to moment the whole being is distressed, deranged, and at last transformed. Had Iago said 'Goats and monkeys!' it would have been no more than the language of the barracks; but for Othello to say it is to return to the jungle and smell its beastliness. Iago's imagery does not rediscover for him his world, as from its dark materials; Othello's world is newly made, from these materials, in every image, and the creative activity is the process of character-making.

XXXII

In the tragedies, then, we see the hero returned to dark and chaotic sources of being, and these sources, not only in a poetical figure, seem to manifest themselves in Nature, in the metaphysical universe, as well as in the soul of man. The generation of images, the fusion in language of imaginative energies into living personality, is a concrete representation, a mimesis, of a human soul in the very process of striving for identity, for ordered vision, in the prolonged encounter between Chaos and Reason, seeking to fashion Chaos into Order. In a profound sense, Macbeth's purpose and problem is not to win and secure the kingdom, not to lend or withhold his ear from his wife's persuasions, not even to accommodate himself to the witches' prophecies—although these are no minor parts of the matter—but to make an identity for himself in language, and even make for himself a universe in language, in the moment-to-moment recognition of those dire constituents of all being—blood, night, sleep, and the existence of a twilight world in which being ceases to be itself.

The encounter, in which the hero seeks identity through the resettlement of vision, is an encounter between the dark energies of the spirit, which seem to have their origins outside the bounds of personality, and those exigencies of time, in which spirit seems obliged to fashion for itself its own redemption or its own destruction. Shakespeare sometimes unmistakably represents for us the significant character of this universal debate. So, on the heath, Lear might seem to be translated out of time, shaping the energies of his personality into terrible apostrophe: but the Fool, cold and shivering, answers with a voice pitifully dictated to by the mere reason of the time:

> Blow, winds, and crack your cheeks! rage! blow!
> You cataracts and hurricanoes, spout
> Till you have drench'd our steeples, drown'd our cocks!
> &c.;

and the Fool—

> O, nuncle, court holy-water in a dry house is better than this rain-water out of doors;

and Lear—

> Rumble thy bellyful! Spit, fire! Spout, rain! &c.;

to which the Fool—

> He that hath a house to put his head in has a good head-piece.

This is a terrible and pitiful controversy between the dark passion of the soul and the immediate recommendation of the rigours of the time. And, of course, the interplay between the language of time and the language that speaks for a world out of time marks the speech of the tragic character himself, making a shaping dialectic within the work of the imagery. So Lear in the midst of those apostrophes, in which his whole personality seeks to reckon with the elements, remembers his daughters and calls those elements 'servile ministers' because they conspire with these daughters against a head 'so old and white' as his. We might say, reinterpreting Aristotle, that there is terror for that which is out of time, and pity for that which is in time, and they make a single experience.

V

TRAGEDY AND THE
'KINGDOM OF ENDS'

XXXIII

THERE is, I believe, a logical connexion—I will not say, development—discernible in the three great tragedies, in terms of which Shakespeare is seen to treat this debate between that which is temporal and that which is metaphysical, in three different modes. One mode was to set side by side in the play, separate from each other, secular society—as it is apprehended in the comedies and, perhaps, the histories but seen now as 'immoral'—and a single human soul. This is done in *Othello*. A second mode was to follow the single human soul into the darkness, where reality and morality are cancelled, and where the soul seeks but never finds identity in the dark recesses of his own being. This is done in *Macbeth*. A final and supreme mode was to see that world in which the hero seeks identity as wholly involved with the life of society, and to move for a moment towards the vision of a kind of identity which comes to men when they are members of each other. This is done in *King Lear*.

XXXIV

In the opening scenes of *Othello* the sense of society is strongly emphasized. Othello lives and loves in a society as particularized, as concrete, as the society depicted in *The Merchant of Venice*. It is much the same kind of society, too; its values and behaviours are of the same sort, they belong to the same Venice. But they are no longer seen *from within*, but from without, and hence differently. They themselves come up now for judgement. It is a society, indeed, which has also something in common with the society of *Measure for Measure*. Natural man is similarly at odds with social order, and there is a licence in men's conduct which social disapproval barely contains and privily condones. It is this sense of a particular and restricted society which gives to *Othello* a general quality different from that of *Macbeth* or *King Lear*; something not so grand, something less universal in its range. In *Othello* we are aware of a human community closely contained within its own meannesses, hypocrisies, and greeds. Part of the tragedy consists in the reduction of the large spirit of Othello to the petty dimensions of the society in which he moves.

Professor Wilson Knight has suggested that one of the notable things about this play is the separateness of the 'worlds' in which the major characters live. And superficially, perhaps, it looks as though Iago's world is quite opaque to Desdemona's and Desdemona's to Othello's. But only superficially. Surely Desdemona and Iago belong to the same world, to the same Venice. Desdemona is not less truly Brabantio's daughter than Roderigo is Iago's dupe. I think she has been imagined as a citizen of that world. This does not mean that she must be full citizen as perhaps Iago is. It means, rather, that her world implies Iago's world and Iago's hers.

For there is little relation between Othello's valuation of fidelity and hers. She takes her valuation from that very same world in which Iago has turned cynic. His cynicism is the natural corollary of her innocence, and they belong to the same level of human being. Her innocence has, indeed, as little true spiritual value— it has a like charm—as Eve's before the Fall.

There is, however, a significant separateness of 'worlds' in *Othello*; it is the separateness of Othello's world from that to which all the other characters equally belong. In an earlier section I pointed out the difference between Othello's world and Iago's. It must now be suggested that Iago's world is the world of Venice, to which all the Venetians were born and in which they were imagined. It is more than that. It is society as Shakespeare now presented it. The central recommendation of society, so conceived, is cynically summed up in Iago's 'Put money in thy purse'. It is a world in which soldiers compete for office and prestige. It is a world in which, as Emilia well knows, men will do each other's officer in the women's beds. It is a world in which lust flaunts its finery and is not abashed. It is a world, indeed, from which spirit has been drained, and all is measured by use and entertainment and position. It is a kingdom of means, not ends.

We do not judge this society by any standard to which any actual society might attain. We do not set against it an ideal society towards which an actual society might asymptotically move. In judging the society in this Venice, we make a judgement on the very nature of all society whatsoever. We see that this society is, in fact, representative of society in general; and that society in general sets up use against value, expediency against integrity, prestige against principle, behaviour against moral being. In *Othello*, two worlds are set in opposition: the world set in time and inhabited by the Venetians; the world of the spirit, in terms of which we apprehend Othello. For this reason, in the bulk of the play, these Venetians are seen by Shakespeare from the outside, they are seen as they behave; whereas Othello is seen from within, he is seen as he is.

Othello is, in one respect, an extremely simple play, for the conflict between 'value' and 'use' is set out in its most extreme terms. Othello, in his deepest spirit, knows very little of use; Iago nothing of value. Othello's thought and feeling at the beginning of the play are free from the pressures of temporal things; they have a purity and spontaneity which remind us of an early innocence. There is a sense, indeed, in which Othello is at first imagined as without original sin, and self-regarding impulses in him are not yet touched with guilt, but —so undivided is he from the world he makes for himself—these very impulses are transmuted and (to speak in Christian terms) of themselves turn God-ward. They are naturally innocent.

In *Othello*, indeed, is re-enacted the Fall of Man; and Othello himself has that superiority of spiritual being

over Desdemona which Adam had over Eve. Iago is the
Tempter, but in conspiracy with him is all Venice and
all the Venetians. They very aptly make that world
within which fallen man confined himself. Othello is
brought by Iago—and, perhaps in another way, by
Desdemona—to indulge himself, to surrender himself
to self-regarding impulses which are all infected and
diseased by the meaner expectations and vanities which
society may breed in our flesh. He becomes subject to
the very itches of the flesh, and jealousy degrades his love
so that it becomes no more than lust. As to Adam, so to
Othello, 'Chaos is come again'. Hoodwinked by Iago,
he leaves the true domain of value and comes down,
shedding all the bravery of his spirit, into Iago's world,
where value is unknown; into Desdemona's world, where
(except through him as by Eve through Adam) value
has never yet been known.

XXXV

Chaos comes indeed to Othello. But what comes after?
What vision does 'character' fulfil at the end of the
play?

Perhaps the first observation we must make, in
answering this question, is that in the closing scene
Othello becomes very much aware of his audience.
Even if it is wrong to accuse him of 'cheering himself up',
it is at least true that he appears to be 'setting himself
right'; and in the process of 'setting himself right' he
seems to lose something of the distinction he once had
and the authority he once exercised amongst the

Venetians. Iago's work, in a measure, has been successful, and Othello has lost both innocence and grace. He
seeks to restore the proper love of himself by recalling
what he has been in the past; and to do this is to come
down to the level of the Venetians. And, of course, he
fails.

But perhaps that is the wrong way to speak of the
matter. After Othello has discovered his fatal error—
and perhaps even before—there is a change in the mode
in which his character is presented. Shakespeare seems
no longer to 'dart himself forth'. He seems, indeed, to
have ceased altogether that kind of character-creation
of which I have spoken earlier in this essay—when, in
language, a human soul seeks identity in his encounter
with the universe. Othello now seeks no such identity.
Shakespeare presents him; and Othello no longer seems
to be fashioning his identity and settling his vision from
moment to moment in words. He is as he is presented.
The settlement he is making now is with society, not
with the universe. The provenance of the images and
their reinforcement are now to be found in social and
secular experiences and assessments. Rhetoric now
persuades, and no longer reveals. Vision is of a different
kind and employs another mode, a more oblique mode,
of character-presentation. Shakespeare, we may say, is
now outside Othello's spirit and the presentation is now
third-personal. He shows forth Othello to the audience
in a certain light. And this light is secular light, plain
social daylight. Othello is fallen man, indeed, but
Shakespeare—all metaphysical consideration now put

aside—exhibits him, even excuses him, to the social judgement—as though he would say. He has done the state some service, and that is something. He has shown valour in war, and, but for being tried intolerably, he has shown loyalty in love. Some pre-eminence amongst men he must be judged to have had—pre-eminence amongst men.

It was, I have said, Iago's filthy function to bring Othello down to the level of the Venetians. So well does he succeed that at the end of the play it is the social judgement that comes into its own again. Society, we may suppose, is not absolutely represented in Iago. Valour and devoted love are values which society must respect, if it would continue itself. But something has vanished like a dream—the glory and the grandeur of the universe to which we had once thought that Othello had belonged. The tale of fallen man is complete, and, for my part, I find here as yet no hint of regeneration or redemption.

XXXVI

Not one of the central images in *Macbeth* is regulative; not one steadies us for life in society. And this can be said of no other of Shakespeare's plays. In *Othello* we are continually reminded in Cassio, in Iago, even in Othello himself by image and idea of a world of social obligation and expectation. In *King Lear* order in society is apprehended with the same actuality as the threat of chaos, whether in society or the individual. It is true that in *Othello* the accepted, the external, world is hard and harsh with cynicism and the test of use, but we never lose the sense of the actuality of that world. And in *Lear* the animal imagery is balanced and criticized by the images of clothes. Bestial individualism is set against the needs and imperatives of life in civilized society. But in *Macbeth* we are never so steadied by inescapable reminders from the actual world, and we lose the sense of that ethical and political order which is expressed in social institutions.

It was inevitable, then, that at least one of the central images should be the image of blood, for blood is the symbol both of life and death, the principle of energy within. It has deep significance in sacrifice and sacrament. The pulse of the blood sets the rhythm of our beings, and its movement records and expresses every chance and change of the spirit. Both joy and horror affect it; and the dry skin or the parched lips are only secondary appearances of these affections of the blood. There could be no other image which so strikingly marked that moment in the development of Shakespeare's vision in which, with all its implications, he saw and imagined the workings of the human spirit absolutely from within.

The image recurs time and again in *Macbeth*. Duncan's first words are:

> What bloody man is that?

Lady Macbeth calls upon the spirits 'that tend our mortal thoughts':

> Make thick my blood.

She bids her husband

> smear
>
> The sleepy grooms with blood.

But Macbeth looks at his hangman's hands and cries out:

> Will all great Neptune's ocean wash the blood
> Clean from my hand?

Lennox cries of the murdered grooms:

> Their hands and faces were all badged with blood,

and of Duncan it is said:

> His silver skin lac'd with his golden blood.

During the banquet scene Macbeth speaks much of blood:

> Blood hath been shed ere now.

> It will have blood; they say, blood will have blood.

> I am in blood
>
> Stepp'd in so far that, should I wade no more,
> Returning were as tedious as go o'er.

And, towards the end, Lady Macbeth walks in her sleep, making as though she would wash her hands;

> Yet who would have thought the old man to have had so much blood in him?

> Here's the smell of blood still.

With the evocation of these images the social sense has nothing to do.

Similarly there are many images of night and sleep. These again are not regulative or descriptive; they evoke in us the very act of annihilating real and solid things, of making blurred the outlines of objects, of mantling the surfaces with darkness. Lady Macbeth calls on night in her opening soliloquy:

> Come, thick night,
> And pall me in the dunnest smoke of hell,
> That my keen knife see not the wound it makes,
> Nor heaven peep through the blanket of the dark,
> To cry, 'Hold, hold'.

At night reality loses its noted order;

> The night has been unruly; where we lay,
> Our chimneys were blown down.
>   . . . the obscure bird
> Clamour'd the livelong night.

The murder of Duncan is done near midnight. Throughout the third act of the play we expect the night.

> Come, seeling night,
> Scarf up the tender eye of pitiful day;
> And with thy bloody and invisible hand
> Cancel and tear to pieces that great bond
> Which keeps me pale! Light thickens; and the crow
> Makes wing to the rooky wood;
> Good things of day begin to droop and drowse
> While night's black agents to their preys do rouse.

Before night comes, but with night in the air, Banquo is murdered;

> The west yet glimmers with some streaks of day.

And something of the common experience of nightfall is reported in the words of the first murderer:

> Now spurs the lated traveller apace
> To gain the timely Inn.

When the guests have left the banquet-hall, Macbeth asks:

> What is the night?

And Lady Macbeth tells him:

> Almost at odds with morning, which is which.

The witches belong to the night; they are 'secret, black and midnight hags'. And it is at night, fearfully, that Lady Macbeth walks in her sleep.

I find it difficult to set down the significance of the images of sleep. In sleep the spirit returns to its elemental resting-place and in a natural rhythm the energies are given pause. In sleep, too, reality is suspended and its demands on us are for the time being quiet. But there may be, too, a sleep which is no sleep but a waking, when the spirit is troubled, and wayward impulses find speech and chance expression. Sleep of this kind is a twilight kingdom, in which we dwell with things half-real. The images of sleep, then, in *Macbeth*, have not a simple but a complex significance. They are an expression of the half-wish to cancel reality; they show within the very anarchy of energy a nostalgia for rest. They represent that ultimate abrogation of the external world in which either the untroubled heart is at rest or else the troubled spirit stirs and mutters and is afraid.

For Macbeth there is to be no more the sweetness of sleep;

> Methought I heard a voice cry, 'Sleep no more!
> Macbeth doth murder sleep!'

And this sleep is 'innocent', it is a

> Sleep that knits up the ravell'd sleave of care,
> The death of each day's life, sore labour's bath,
> Balm of hurt minds, great nature's second course,
> Chief nourisher in life's feast.

Duncan knows such a sleep in death;

> Wake Duncan with thy knocking! I would thou couldst.

> > Duncan is in his grave:
> After life's fitful fever he sleeps well.

At the end of the banquet scene Lady Macbeth says to her husband:

> You lack the season of all natures, sleep.

And Macbeth replies:

> Come, we'll to sleep.

We remember all this of sleep when Macbeth asks of the doctor,

> Canst thou not minister to a mind diseased,
> Pluck from the memory a rooted sorrow,
> Raze out the written troubles of the brain,
> And with some sweet oblivious antidote
> Cleanse the stuff'd bosom of that perilous stuff
> Which weighs upon the heart?

Terror and unrest come, too, with these images of sleep, as though in sleep this perilous stuff may have at its mercy the deeps of the spirit and all the mind. Banquo first mentions this helplessness in sleep, when he says:

> And yet I would not sleep; merciful powers,
> Restrain in me the cursed thoughts that nature
> Gives way to in repose!

The grooms must have been disturbed by dreams, when one laughed in his sleep and one cried 'Murder!' After the murder, Macbeth will risk anything rather than

> sleep
> In the affliction of these terrible dreams
> That shake us nightly.

Lady Macbeth in 'a most fast sleep' rises from her bed, throws her nightgown upon her, takes forth paper, writes upon it, reads it, afterwards seals it, and again returns to bed.

Nothing in the play is what it seems; nothing belongs to its own 'law of kinde'. In *Macbeth*, 'fair is foul and foul is fair'; pleasantly-sited castles are the settings for dreadful murder;

> by the clock, 'tis day,
> And yet dark night strangles the travelling lamp;

a man may be not of woman born; and Birnam Wood can come to Dunsinane.

This leads me to mention the emphasis laid in the play on phantasmal experience, on illusion, on half-appearance. The energy of inner imagining seems very often to be too much for solid reality; and the world of Macbeth becomes a world of shadows, of visitations from a space other than this. The eye conjures beings out of the very air; and things real dissolve into unreality. Neither the eye nor the ear can be wholly believed and all assurance is lost.

Banquo asks of the witches:

> I' the name of truth,
> Are ye fantastical, or that indeed
> Which outwardly ye show?

And when they have vanished he says:

> The earth hath bubbles, as the water has,
> And these are of them. Whither are they vanished?

Macbeth gives him his answer:

> Into the air; and what seemed corporeal melted
> As breath into the wind.

Certainly the dagger which Macbeth sees before he goes in to murder Duncan is 'fantastical'. When he would clutch it, he clutches empty air. He has it and he has it not. It is 'a dagger of the mind, a false creation', and yet it is in form as 'palpable' as that which now he draws. In the 'dagger' soliloquy, the images of sleep and the images of dreams are joined with fantastical imaginings—and with night:

> Now o'er the one half world
> Nature seems dead, and wicked dreams abuse
> The curtained sleep; witchcraft celebrates
> Pale Hecate's offerings, and withered murder,
> Alarum'd by his sentinel, the wolf,
> Whose howl's his watch, thus with his stealthy pace,
> With Tarquin's ravishing strides, towards his design,
> Moves like a ghost.

XXXVII

What has all this to do with character? In the first place, we can surely say that what goes on in Macbeth's mind when he fears that he will sleep no more, when he knows that 'blood will have blood', when Nature in half the world seems dead to him, is just as revealing, though differently, as the practical question which he puts to himself: Shall I kill a king? We can say more: we can say that killing a king would be a small and merely public matter, were it not that to kill a king involves Macbeth in less palpable encounters, which find their mimesis in the poetry. To kill a king was the first act— and what followed may be thought of as a catalogue of crimes, but, more truly, is apprehended as an ever closer encounter with darkness.

Early in the play Macbeth is in some doubt: he hesitates on the very brink of action. The theme of his soliloquy, 'If it were done, &c.', is the theme of 'judgement here', something that has to do not with moral conscience, but with the fear of consequences. This fear has puzzled a large number of critics in the past, and if we inquire, What is it Macbeth really fears? we shall be hard put to it to find an answer. One would not suppose that he fears physical punishment. By his own hypothesis he does not fear death. What then? The answer is that he fears nothing in particular. He fears that unknown chain of consequences which (once we think of them) may make us tremble before any act whatsoever. The fear phrases itself but does not define itself for Macbeth as a judgement, as the return of the poisoned chalice to his own lips. But the fear is, in fact, something fundamental and more deeply rooted in the general condition of man; it is the fear, or the distrust, or the moral uncertainty, which attaches itself to any act whatsoever. It is precisely the same fear which prevented Hamlet from killing the king. It is the Either/Or of our human being.

But in *Macbeth* the matter is a little different. The play is not a play about doubt or indecision; it is a play about those ineluctable processes which follow decision. It is not irrelevant to point out here that Shakespeare deliberately distorted the historical facts. The historical Macbeth reigned well, as far as we know, for ten years after the murder. Our Macbeth is from the moment of the act an exile from the daylight. We can be sure, then, that Shakespeare, as by way of supreme experiment, takes as the hypothesis of his play an extreme case of a man's delivery of himself, through action, to darkness, to chaos. Macbeth, as a tragic hero, is a man with a capacity, one might almost say a taste, for damnation. This capacity, as Mr. Eliot once pointed out, is not so very different from a capacity for salvation. *Macbeth* is a terrible play because its business is to give us some notion of what that damnation is which a man embraces when he is, indeed, man enough for it.

Whereas in *Othello* we witness the Fall of Man, in *Macbeth* we have a study (not, as Mr. Stewart would have us suppose, of a man) of Fallen Man; Man, who, because he is fallen, cannot reject the discipline of daylight without involving himself in utter darkness. And how vision reveals itself in *Macbeth* may be conveniently illustrated from the two main soliloquies in the play, one at the beginning, the other at the end. In the soliloquy just mentioned, when Macbeth hesitates before the act, order (the order of civil institutions and decent hospitalities) is still actual for him. He remembers that Duncan is his king, his kinsman, and his guest. In the same speech he remembers 'virtue' and 'angels' and 'heaven's cherubin'; and although I do not think these argue a Christian 'philosophy' in the play, they do at least indicate that Macbeth is not yet committed to the darkness. Something still tells him that 'institutions are necessary', and, although he does not say so, necessary perhaps to salvation. Towards the end of the play—the hypothesis has worked itself out—all sense of actuality and order is lost. Life has become 'a tale told by an idiot, full of sound and fury, signifying nothing'.

But vision does not rest there, for while Shakespeare may not here affirm Divine Order, he certainly could not accept a godless existentialism. This is as far as vision, discovering itself in and through Macbeth, could go; but now it changes its mode, as it does at the end of *Othello*. In these last moments Macbeth, not perhaps for himself but for us, is brought back to the daylight world. Social order, daylight order, reasserts itself. He himself admits that the juggling fiends have paltered with him in a double sense, and, as he confesses this, he opens his eyes to the world and to his audience. He becomes a man once again behaving in the presence of men, and that is how Shakespeare represents him. One social virtue he can still exhibit, not redeeming him, but giving him distinction and pre-eminence—the virtue of courage, however desperately called upon. His vision no longer matters, except in so far as we judge it and find it wanting. But his courage matters, for men should be brave. And yet, in a sense, it is wrong to say that his vision no longer matters: for through it we have been brought to the edge of nothingness and dissolution. And it is as men who have been so near that edge that we hear at last the mention of 'measure, time, and place'.

XXXVIII

King Lear is the play in which Shakespeare returns once again to see man as a human soul, not in opposition to society, not rejecting society, but finding in society the sphere of fulfilment. Order is now seen, for the first time, and perhaps imperfectly, 'not merely negative, but creative and liberating'. It is a vision of society very different from that discovered in *Othello*. In *Othello* we cannot suppose that society is ever moral or good. Othello and Iago die, but future Othellos will find themselves betrayed in Venice, and future Iagos will still prey upon its profligates. In *King Lear* the conflict is no longer apprehended as a conflict between the individual and society; the conflict is now within society itself. Disorder in the human soul is both the agent and the product of disorder in society. Social order is the condition, as it is the resultant, of sweet and affirmative being, without which man relapses into a beastly and self-destructive individualism.

The play gives an impression of towns and villages and castles, on which the barren moor and the wild marshland are ever ready to encroach. Outside the walls lies the realm of brutishness, of animals and roots, of standing pools and naked madmen. Certain of the characters become exiles from comfort, from decent living, from politeness. Lear, in the wind and the rain and the thunder, and in the hovel, is such an exile. So is Edgar, in the rags of Tom o'Bedlam. So are the fool and, afterwards, the blind Gloucester. The beastly life is very close, near neighbour to civilized man; and man has not much to do to resume the life of the beast.

He has only to cast off his clothes—for in this symbolism Shakespeare dramatically anticipates Carlyle. Clothes alone divide men from the animals:

Is man no more than this? Consider him well. Thou owest the worm no silk, the beast no hide, the sheep no wool, the cat no perfume. Ha! here's three on's are sophisticated! Thou art the thing itself: unaccommodated man is no more but such a poor, bare, forked animal as thou art: Off, off, you lendings! Come, unbutton here.

And when Lear flings off his clothes we may remember his words to Regan earlier in the play:

O, reason not the need: our basest beggars
Are in the poorest thing superfluous:
Allow not nature more than nature needs,
Man's life is cheap as beast's: thou art a lady;
If only to go warm were gorgeous,
Why, nature needs not what thou gorgeous wear'st,
Which scarcely keeps thee warm.

Brutish nature is made actual for us in the frequent mention of animals, especially those who prey upon each other. And disorder in humanity is symbolized in rank and wayward weeds which seem ever to encroach on the cultivated field.

The imagery of clothes—and many other things in the play—reinforce the notion that in society 'institutions are necessary'; and character in the play is certainly conceived in terms of social rank and function, as well as in terms of the family. We expect trouble, indeed, when at the beginning of the play we learn that Lear intends to continue rank without function, has subscribed his power, and confined it merely to 'exhibition', and would manage those 'authorities' which he has given away. The bastardy of Edmund ('there was good sport at his making') has such results that we see a 'fault', where a woman has 'a son for her cradle ere she [has] a husband for her bed'. Ironically enough, it is an insistence on the rightness and reasonableness of institutions which gives some point to the sisters' complaint that Lear's hundred retainers are intolerably more than 'nature' needs. There is nothing in the play to cast suspicion upon the rightness of external order—there is much in the play to make us feel that without it we are lost, to affirm that not discipline, but indiscipline destroys. But there is also much to support the view that even discipline will destroy where it is not involved in self-discipline and in love.

King Lear—this is a large claim to make—is the only one of Shakespeare's plays in which personal relationship is treated as an end and not as a means; the only play in which personal relationships seem to determine character rather than to have an effect upon character. It is not merely that, say, in *Hamlet* the relationships between Hamlet and his mother and Hamlet and Ophelia are subsidiary in the major vision of the play; it is rather that what these characters are, and especially Hamlet, in his personal relationships, is important and enriches the vision, but the relationship in itself plays no necessary part in that vision and is incidental to it.[1] We may think that Ophelia's kind of love is a betrayal and that Hamlet's spirit is the more embittered: but what concerns us is not that Hamlet should have loved Ophelia but that by love he should be so embittered. In *King Lear*, however, all the characters are conceived —and this is central to the vision—in their relationships with other people, in their relationships with each other, and society is a vital complex of such relationships. In *King Lear*, then, not only is individual character differently conceived, but also living society itself.

The question is one of priority, not psychological but imaginative. In *Hamlet* (to continue the example) the nature of personal relationship is dependent on the nature of the characters: in *King Lear*, in a large measure, the nature of the character is revealed in the personal relationship. In *Hamlet* relationship and character are separable: in *King Lear* they are wholly bound up with each other. So it is that in *King Lear* personal relationships are the field of character-fulfilment.

[1] Family relationships are not the same, of course, as personal relationships.

None other of Shakespeare's plays contains such moving and dramatic references to personal loyalty and love. This play opens with the grand and, perhaps, grotesque announcement of the major theme in Lear's demand that his daughters shall declare their love. I do not find this opening difficult to accept; it is a bold enlargement of that morbidity which can poison affection, when affection gives nothing and asks everything. Lear's need to be told is matched by the two elder daughters' readiness in the telling; and it is seen, not wholly but in part, for what it is, in Cordelia's inability to tell. There follow immediately many variations of the theme; for Burgundy personal relationship is a matter of use, whereas to the King of France it is a matter of value. Kent is loyal, Goneril and Regan whisper together because, for a while, their interests are in common. The King of France finds words for the theme, when he says:

> Love is not love
> When it is mingled with regards that stand
> Aloof from the entire point.

More subtly and more movingly, Cordelia's conduct quickens and illuminates the vision; for her love, which cannot speak, has some regards—she cannot help it—which stand 'aloof from the *entire* point'. She is to blame, although she can do no other, for keeping herself blameless.

There is no need to rehearse the way in which Shakespeare deepens and develops this vision in the creation of his characters in *King Lear*. One or two of the minor characters catch a vivid if momentary life from it. I think of the servant who bids Cornwall hold his hand:

> I have served you ever since I was a child,
> But better service have I never done you
> Than now to bid you hold.

Or of the old man who brings the blinded Gloucester to Edgar:

> O my good lord!
> I have been your tenant, and your father's tenant,
> These fourscore years.

Such a man sweetens and fortifies institutions with loyalty and service. Loyalty is found in Oswald, too—and in Kent. Lear himself—although this is too large a matter to do more than hint at—insists on his hundred followers, but comes to the moment when he bids the fool go first into the hovel; thinks of 'poor naked wretches'; will make a little society of affection in prison with Cordelia; thanks a gentleman for undoing his button. And is not something darker suggested, related to this same vision, when the two sisters both desire Edmund?

> Yet Edmund was belov'd;
> The one the other poison'd for my sake
> And after slew herself.

The weeds, after all, spring from the same soil as the 'sustaining corn'.

Personal relationships, however, are conceived in two ways—in loyalty and consideration which are owed according merely to the 'bond', and in that going out of oneself which makes of love and loyalty something more than is demanded by the bond. So, in the first Act, Lear does a terrible thing to Cordelia; he inhibits in her that love which has no need of a bond. So we apprehend that moral behaviours are inseparably bound up with each other, hers with his, for it is Lear who puts Cordelia in the position of relying merely on the bond. In similar fashion, Kent's honesty shows a loyalty something more than his commitment—and this honesty has in it a bluntness something more than the mere requirement of its occasion. There is, indeed, throughout the play a deep sense of the evil that must mix with goodness—and of the 'reason' that may mix with evil; and Shakespeare makes it clear that the admixture of good with evil, of evil with 'reason', is both proof and product of the fact that, morally, we are members of each other. There is, indeed, in *King Lear*, a kind of irony which is not, to any important extent, to be found in any other play: the irony which lies in the contradiction between the rightness of what is said and the wrongness of its being said by that particular character, or in that particular situation, or in that particular manner. Lear is old, and his age is full of changes, but his daughters should not say so. There is no reply—no reply but 'Nothing'—to Lear's request that Cordelia should outdo her sisters in protestation of her love; but Cordelia should not make that reply. Kent should warn the king, but loyalty asks for more mannerly phrasing. The vision that is discovered in character in the early part of the play is that vision which sees, in all its complexities, the play in

conduct of mere 'reason' and 'rightness', at odds with
that other play of something more than 'reason', something more than 'rightness'. So much is this the theme of
the first Act that we may risk the judgement that this is
what the play is about. Nature, we are to learn, needs
more than reason gives.

Except for the King of France, the first Act shows all
the other characters—this is the manner in which they
were conceived—determining their conduct and their
speech either by self-regarding 'reason' or by a sense of
'rightness' which has in it something of self-regard. At
any rate, conduct in them is determined, in one way or
another, according merely to the need or the letter, and,
because of this, has in it an admixture of evil and necessary
imperfection. Whether the regard for self be 'proper' or
'improper', at the beginning of the play the impulse in
conduct is almost universally self-regarding, or has in it
something self-regarding as a presiding element. Something in self, something inhibitory in the conduct of
another combining with something in self, prevents a
'going out' of the self. Even where the spirit is generous,
it is forced to seek refuge in 'reason', in the letter, and is
thereby frustrated and impoverished. At the end of the
play, however, conduct—again in one way or another
—becomes something more than 'reason' needs. There
is, for example, a kind of generosity, a certain 'going out'
of the self, in Goneril, when she says, 'I have been worth
the whistle'. There is, in this, release from the self, and
much more than 'reason' needs. So, too, in Edmund's
'Yet Edmund was belov'd'; and it is significant that this

is followed immediately by something very much like remorse for others. Edmund—and Goneril, too, for that matter—shows himself for a moment as man enough to be damned. When Lear thinks of the 'poor naked wretches', there is a most subtle play on all these themes —for such compassion in him has been in the past more than reason has seemed to need and is now a 'going out' of himself; and yet in this compassion there is a higher reason, which shows the heavens 'more just'. Reason and compassion come together at last, when Kent says of the king:

> Vex not his ghost: O! let him pass; he hates him
> That would upon the rack of this rough world
> Stretch him out longer.

And, a little later:

> I have a journey, sir, shortly to go;
> My master calls me, I must not say no.

The movement of the play seems to be from conduct (and character) in which reason is governed by self-regard, to conduct (and character) in which reason is transformed by compassion. In an image, this compassion becomes a healing and medicinal balm. So the third servant says of Gloucester:

> I'll fetch some flax and whites of eggs
> To apply to his bleeding face.

And Cordelia of her father:

> O my dear father! Restoration hang
> Thy medicine on my lips, and let this kiss

Repair those violent harms that my two sisters
Have in thy reverence made!

That was one way of representing compassion.

'Institutions are necessary', but they are administered by men, and, necessary though they are, they are no guarantee against viciousness and evil. Lear, in his madness, has a terrible picture of what may lie beneath the façade of social and political institutions, and for a moment we have a vision of all society itself, in its forms and customs, rotten and hypocritical. It is a picture of society in which institutions are all false-seeming, and justice itself is so perverted that it lends itself as a disguise to those very ills on which it passes judgement. The image of clothes is still used by Shakespeare:

Through tatter'd clothes small vices do appear;
Robes and furred gowns hide all.

Here is society, as Lear in his madness sees it, without grace, without sweetness. The law conceals what it cannot prevent, and, by stealth, luxury goes to it, pell-mell. As we envisage such a society, we have a physical nausea, which makes us wish, like Lear, 'an ounce of civet' to sweeten our imaginations. We have raised the stone and seen the maggots. Shakespeare never gave us a clearer clue—and there is another in that travesty of justice as Lear arraigns the joint-stools in the hovel—to the vision of the play from which the characters draw their identities.

But it is not a merely secular society in which these characters are conceived to have their being. Nor, on the other hand, do I think it can be said (even through allegory) to be a society understood in terms of Christian theology. Nevertheless, to put the matter quite simply, we certainly get the impression in the play that the characters are imagined not only as members of each other but also as members of a Nature which is active both within themselves and throughout the circumambient universe. Man is nowhere so certainly exhibited as a member of all organic creation and of the elemental powers. Man's membership of society is more than legal, is more than political, because it is subtended in a wider membership, in which plants and animals, the wind and the thunder, are also included. And is it too extravagant to suggest that this natural universe is, in the earlier part of the play, peopled not only by men but also by beings of a primitive pagan belief—by Hecate, by Apollo, by Jupiter, by 'the gods'; and that the dominion of these beings is, in the action of the play, superseded? Is it, indeed, too extravagant to suggest that in the play we have a veritable change in dispensation? That, at any rate, is the impression given as the imagery changes and one store of images gives way to another. What the final dispensation is, however, it is difficult to determine, for Shakespeare seems not to specify it. The most we can say is that, like the promise of rain in Mr. T. S. Eliot's *The Waste Land*, there are moments and images towards the end of *King Lear* which give promise of grace and benediction.

XXXIX

It is hard, then, to understand how *King Lear* can ever have been taken to be 'the most Senecan of all Shakespeare's tragedies'. Even Mr. Eliot, while seeking to suggest that there is 'much less and much more' than Senecan Stoicism in the play, agrees that 'there is [in it] a tone of Senecan fatalism; *fatis agimur*'. I should have thought that of all Shakespeare's tragedies this statement is least true of *King Lear*. It cannot be argued, surely, that we are to take as true for the whole play Gloucester's statement:

> As flies to wanton boys, are we to the gods:
> They kill us for their sport.

The characters seem to me to be self-active and responsible, and even the idea that 'ripeness is all' is scarcely resignation as Seneca might have understood it. What might be mistaken for resignation is, indeed, something very different, and not at all Senecan; I mean the humility which manifests itself unmistakably in Lear, in Edgar, in Albany, at the end of the play. Goneril's 'I have been worth the whistle' and Edmund's 'Yet Edmund was belov'd' have in them something of the element which Mr. Eliot has called 'cheering oneself up'; but they are more than that. Moreover, these utterances come too late, in a moment too desperate, for them to be dismissed merely as the speech of Pride. Not Pride, indeed, but Humility, which is the 'reverse' of the stoical attitude, is the most memorable principle at the end of the play; but we could never have known what this

Humility was, had we not learned also something about Pride. True humility, moreover, goes hand in hand with compassion, and so it is in the closing scenes of *King Lear*. Does not the play look forward to Dostoievsky, rather than back to Seneca?

XL

In general, the tragic hero is conceived as pursuing a settlement not only with secular society but also with his universe. Settlement with society is not enough; for he must also find for himself an identity which, while giving him mastery over his temporal problems, justifies that mastery with a more than temporal sanction. The nature of his settlement with his universe is determined in the pursuit of settlement itself. In this sense it is true to say that Shakespeare had no 'philosophy'. It is no prefabricated universe with which the hero seeks to find accommodation; it is no prefabricated universe which at his peril and cost he ignores. The Christian categories never preside over the vision, although, naturally enough, the vision is impregnated with Christian sentiment. Tragedy finds its origin not in a Christian idea of imperfection but in 'Renaissance anarchism'.

Only through grace, perhaps, if at all, can man find blessedness; and Shakespearian tragedy is tragedy simply because in it Fallen Man seeks to find rehabilitation in 'infiniteness'—but without grace. The tragedy is in the failure, and perhaps the failure is general to the case of Man. The tragic character (and in this there is no Senecan 'cheering oneself up') will not resign himself to confinement in the secular world; but he has no certitude of status in a world more absolute. We cannot judge the tragic character in terms of our temporal moralities; neither can we schematize those mysteries of redemption which might at last exempt him from such judgements. He believes that he belongs to this world and he believes that he does not. He would jump the life to come—and yet he dare not. He comes to know that 'the readiness is all', but that same ripeness, which releases him from the importunities of this world, discovers for him no other. Shakespearian tragedy is the product of the change in men's minds—the Renaissance change—by which men came to feel themselves separate from God; by which, indeed, the idea of God receded from men's habitual certitudes and became no more and often less than an intellectual construction, a merely credible hypothesis, a Being remote and not certainly just or beneficent, perhaps the Enemy. In a world where anarchism was of recent development and men had not yet resigned themselves to a disabling opportunism man's perennial hunger for metaphysical being prompted Shakespeare to create supreme drama out of the question, How shall man find the intersection between that which is in time and that which is out of time? Or, to put the matter simply, and I do not think too simply, What shall we do to be saved?

VI

ORDER AND CONTINUANCE IN SOCIETY

XLI

NEITHER Antony nor Cleopatra is exempt at any time from the social judgement. Not the gods but Caesar says of Antony and Cleopatra that never in death were 'clipped' a pair 'so famous'. Caesar was a man, and these two are famous amongst men. Not before the gods but amongst men was Coriolanus, for courage and soldiership, pre-eminent. Not to the universe but to society are we concerned to accommodate what these men were. It is, indeed, a little extravagant to use words such as 'mystery' and 'value', when we discuss how lust and martial valour are treated in these plays. After all, pre-eminence in bed or on the battlefield command a social admiration, even while they may make us a little uncomfortable. And it is on these different attitudes that these characters play: it is out of these attitudes that they are largely wrought. Vision is not discovered by our looking at the world through Antony's eyes or by our addressing the world as Coriolanus addressed it. Rather is it true to say that Antony's world-view and Coriolanus's world-attitude are matters which vision has to reckon with—and this is a reckoning which involves no 'going out of ourselves', no becoming in and for some other 'being'. We never

feel either the sins or the sufferings of Antony and
Coriolanus to be ours as well as theirs.

In neither play does the imagery create for us a
circumambient universe, although in the imagery a con-
ventional universe, both physical and metaphysical, is
taken for granted. Every image seems to come authorized
and processed (as it were) by social and literary usage.
Language never returns, for however short a time, to the
unconditioned places of its origins. And this is true of
the supreme moments of the play—true, for example, of
Cleopatra's 'Husband, I come'. Because the imagery is
what it is, shaped and substantiated by social and literary
usage, the characters never fashion for themselves their
world or their universe; they speak and behave within
a world and a universe already fashioned. In this respect,
Caesar and Antony have no disagreement.

It will be useful to look a little more closely at Cleopatra's use of the word 'husband', for it will give us a
clue to the extraordinary potency of language in poetic
drama, as well as to the relation between language and
'character'. Here, indeed, is language *feliciter audax*; and
the 'happy valiancy' would never have been achieved,
if language had had to express the same scope and
seriousness of vision which mark the great tragedies.
Some critics would have us believe that Cleopatra 'vindi-
cates her right to Antony's devotion' when she says,

> Husband, I come:
> Now to that name my courage prove my title.

Professor Peter Alexander, for example, supposes that
the scene in which Cleopatra dies is a ritual which

'makes visible to the eye of sense the mystery of their union'. I cannot believe that this scene is any such matter. The truth is that Cleopatra takes leave (and we allow her leave) to make believe in death that their union was other than it was. There was something in the union, certainly, which gives her now a temporary title to call Antony her husband; but what this something was is no mystery. It was that kind of physical surrender and fulfilment which 'continuates' society, and to which society (without dealing in 'mystery') gives, at the very heart of disapproval, admiration. For, in Antony and Cleopatra, this surrender and fulfilment, though of its own kind absolute, did not 'continuate' society; and that it did not gives a special and poignant irony to these other words of the queen:

> Peace! Peace!
> Dost thou not see my baby at my breast,
> That sucks the nurse asleep?

Pity now licenses our admiration, and disapproval is so subdued that we can make the sublime pretence that this union was not as it was, but otherwise.

Not even here—not anywhere—is Cleopatra really self-transcendent. And the same judgement must be made of Antony and Coriolanus. We do not see the universe through their eyes; they do not lead us beyond themselves. We see them in the universe and somehow or other within that universe we have to subdue them; to that universe they must, though in death, be reconciled. But in that reconciliation they make no discovery and they experience no transformation of vision.

Neither do we. As in comedy, we wonder how to deal
with them—and then, at the end, we flatter ourselves,
perhaps not unduly, that we knew all the time. So
we build a monument and write an epitaph to com-
memorate a glory that has passed away from the earth.
At an earlier time and in another manner, we did the
same with Falstaff.

In these Roman plays we are never interested in
what these characters do to themselves. On their own
behalf—let us say, as souls to be saved—we never wish
them otherwise. And let us remember that to wish them
otherwise is to wish ourselves, to wish the spiritual
universe, otherwise. For Lear and we are members of
each other. It is not for Antony's sake that we might
wish him active in Rome and it is not for Coriolanus's
sake that we would have him break with the Volscii.
Nor is it for the sake of the spiritual universe. The judgement involved—and I do not see how we can deny that
some such judgement is involved—is a secular and a
social judgement. Let Antony stay in Egypt, he is
neither damned nor redeemed. Let him go to Rome, it
makes no difference. What we miss in these plays, as we
compare them with the other tragedies, is that quality
of humility, which is notable in *King Lear* and which,
I believe, Shakespeare sought after but never quite
achieved in *Macbeth* and *Othello*. The other tragic heroes,
Othello, Macbeth, and Lear, are all men, at one time
or another, capable of humility, and in humility they
would not lose identity. Not so Antony and Coriolanus.
Coriolanus kneels to his mother, but he wins no victory

over himself. It is not in these characters—not so were these characters conceived—to see what they were and what they had been in another light. That kind of vision is left to us; and consequently we may view them with a kind of pity, but not, perhaps, with compassion.

There is one other thing to say about these plays, and it explains, perhaps, the lack of compassion in our attitude to the characters. We can never be sure when there is going to be a hint of levity in the composition; and it is a kind of levity which excludes compassion. It is a levity, too, which marks in Shakespeare's vision some dwindling in the moral status of his heroes—and his heroines; so that one might even say that in them their passion, or their 'humour', is more important than they. The characters of Coriolanus and Cleopatra often come very near to caricature, and even Antony is not exempt from the same treatment. It is as though, from time to time, Shakespeare is half in league with society to denigrate those magnificences of spirit which it must admire but does not easily contain. *Feliciter audax* may be said of Shakespeare's range of sensibility and attitude, as well as of his imagery and his mastery of the stage.

XLII

The date of composition (if the matter may be put as simply as that) of *Troilus and Cressida* has not been certainly established. What follows in this section, therefore, is somewhat doubtfully founded on certain conjectures I made in an article, 'Notes on the Integrity of *Troilus and Cressida*', published in the *Review of English Studies* in April 1943. I suggested that the extant version of *Troilus and Cressida* is a radical revision, made in the year 1608–9, for private performance, of an earlier version, 'acted by my Lord Chamberlain's Men' in 1601–3. My present argument leads to certain considerations about the play which might seem to reinforce that suggestion.

Professor Peter Alexander has written that 'Troilus is to the great tragedies like the anti-masque to the masque, the satyric play to the tragedies it followed'. In this view—and I believe it to be sound—we see in parts of *Troilus and Cressida* a more thoroughgoing and, perhaps, a more self-conscious denigration of those values which society must admire but cannot easily contain. It must be admitted, however, that the play is both masque and anti-masque, something akin to tragedy and satyric play, all in one. The values (I mean of Love and Valour) are both affirmed and denigrated. And, what is just as important, they are debated.

There is a remarkable parallelism of themes between *Troilus* and the Roman plays. Like Antony, not only Troilus but Achilles also finds a conflict between love and duty. Achilles, like Antony, leaves his armour to rust. Cleopatra flirts with Dolabella, and Cressida makes her own sort of truce with Diomed. Cominius, the first of the Romans to seek the return of Coriolanus, comes back with the news: 'He would not seem to know me'. The Greek generals, on the advice of Ulysses, take the initiative in 'strangeness', and pass 'strangely' by Achilles, 'as if he were forgot'. And is not Ajax the base-bred brother of Coriolanus? He 'professes not answering; speaking is for beggars; he wears his tongue in his arms'.

The manifest concern of the play is precisely the same as that of the two Roman plays. Love and Valour are all very well, and without being 'mysteries' they *do* present problems—to reason and to society. In the consideration of these problems *Troilus and Cressida* is notable, not chiefly perhaps for its cynicism, and not chiefly for the power with which passion and honour are realized, but for the energy of common sense which every now and then seems to hold the balance. And in this as in other ways this is the one play by Shakespeare which reminds me of the works of Bernard Shaw, and this would not be surprising, if Shakespeare had devised the play for a private performance, say before the lawyers of the Inns of Court.

For the play is, pre-eminently, a play of ideas. And the method of characterization is the method proper to a play of ideas. The characters are either mouthpieces in the presentation of ideas or else they are embodiments and illustrations or allegories of moments in the argument. The vision that fulfils itself in character is vision articulated beforehand in the form and figure of a problem or a series of problems, and the characters are the translations of the ideas into acting parts, or even, in some cases, into advocates of particular elements in the debate. This accounts for the lack of warmth in the characters, even when there is no lack of verisimilitude. We are interested in the characters, but they do not— not even Troilus or Cressida—command our sympathy.

They have, at another level, something in common with the characters in the plays of Bernard Shaw. Zest and interest and gusto have gone into their making; but no love and little compassion. And the zest and interest and gusto have been excitements of the mind, not of the heart. Is it not, for example, the very trick of such character-making that in Achilles we should see that the 'melancholy' man, the malcontent, may turn out to be no more than a bit of a bounder after all?

It is of the 'malcontent' that Ulysses is thinking, when he says to Achilles:

> . . . no man is the lord of anything,
> Though in and of him there be much consisting,
> Till he communicate his parts to others;
> Nor doth he of himself know them for aught,
> Till he behold them form'd in the applause
> Where they're extended; who, like an arch, reverberates
> The voice again; or, like a gate of steel,
> Fronting the sun, receives and renders back
> His figure and his heat.

This is, indeed, a blast of common sense, aimed at the 'malcontent'. It might be read, too, as a significant gloss on *Coriolanus*, on *Antony*, on *Timon of Athens*—and, curiously enough, on Prospero, who returns in the end to his Dukedom.

XLIII

Although a sound instinct has traditionally placed *Timon of Athens* amongst Shakespeare's minor works, some extravagant judgements have been made upon it

by various critics. Professor Peter Alexander, for example
—although surely right to draw attention to its close
kinship with *Troilus and Cressida*—writes as follows:

> The misanthropy of Apemantus is only the world's self-
> love inside out. But Timon's hate is from no such malice;
> and his occupation is gone not because the citizens will not
> repay their borrowings, but because this refusal wakens him
> from his dream of restoring the golden age and all its
> charities in such a nest of vipers. Apemantus could see the
> world given over to beasts and remain a beast with them,
> but Timon will be man or nothing; and his misanthropy
> comes on him, as it does on the other great misanthrope of
> the stage, because it seems impossible to remain a man
> among his fellows.

Implied within all this is a certain assessment of the
character of Timon and a general interpretation of the
vision of the play. It seems to me that both are in error,
and the argument of this view will, I hope, bring out
more clearly the relationship between character and
vision. (It will be granted that while the 'vision' in a
play may sometimes be very much more than the playwright 'means' it to be, it may also be very much less.)

To begin with Apemantus, whose blood-relationship
with Thersites is unmistakable. If his misanthropy is to
be seen as the 'world's self-love (turned) inside out' (if
his 'character' is to fulfil that kind of 'vision') we must
see something of that 'self-love' dramatically presented.
Considering the pervading tone of the play, this might
have been done in the way Jonson does it in *Volpone*—
that is to say, the self-loving characters might almost

have persuaded us of a world 'given over to beasts' as Jonson's menagerie so persuades us. Jonson's fox, vulture, crow, and raven catch their authentic being from Jonson's moral indignation. Their life is caught from his anger. But Shakespeare's beasts are not beasts at all, because Shakespeare has not even that belief in them which might make him indignant, nor has he that kind of indignation which might make us believe in them. Their self-love (and such beastliness as they have) has all the barrenness of a statistical, and none of the terrible persuasiveness of a universal, possibility. Consequently, Timon's misanthropy (although for the moment we may suppose it psychologically convincing) is artistically and morally disproportionate.

But even psychologically it is unconvincing. Surely Professor Alexander stretches interpretation too far when he says that Timon dreams of 'restoring the golden age' and will be 'a man or nothing'. For the truth is that in the First Act of the play Timon is a fool, and if he dreams at all of restoring the 'golden age', it is the dream of a fool. Why is he a fool? Simply because Shakespeare's vision of a 'golden age', even his vision of 'goodness', is as barren, as factitious, as *statistical*, as his vision of a 'world given over to beasts'. And, as the one vision involves the other, Timon's misanthropy is vitiated by the gross foolishness of his philanthropy. Shakespeare had, of course, virtuosity enough to give to misanthropy effective tongue—and to provide his private audience with an impressive *tour de force*. But what is good and what is evil, although far different in the demands they make on the attention of the social judgement, are as accidental as what is sweet and what is sour, what is rough and what is smooth. Neither the nature of evil nor the nature of goodness is known the better or the more deeply for our reading of *Timon*.

Is it possible, indeed, that what Shakespeare has been able to achieve, whether in poetry or in 'vision', in *Timon*, he was able to achieve partly because, notably in *King Lear* and in *Troilus*, he had, one way or another, done it before? If this is so, it may account for a certain staleness in the writing of the play.

Apemantus is a railer—so was Thersites. Timon, distraught with human ingratitude, turns his back on civil society—so did Lear. In *Timon* loyalty and service bring a little goodness into the play—so do Kent and the old retainer in *Lear*. The Athenians send messengers to Timon to return and save the city—in such a way the Romans sent messengers to Coriolanus.

In doing again what he had, substantially, done before, it was inevitable that Shakespeare should be a little perfunctory, even uninterested, in sustaining a presiding vision in the play. Consequently, it is a play not so much of vision as of situations. Nevertheless, even though it is perfunctorily sustained, there is, if not a presiding, at least a concluding vision, scarcely fulfilling itself in character, but certainly declaring itself in the arrangement of the incidents in which character is engaged. What happens to Timon and what happens to Alcibiades are both variations on the theme already noticed in *Troilus and Cressida*:

> . . . no man is the lord of anything,
> Though in and of him there be much consisting,
> Till he communicate his parts to others.

Timon communicates, not his parts, but his property. He is as much disqualified by his wanton generosity as Achilles is by his churlishness. And neither was the 'lord of anything'. Similarly, Alcibiades becomes himself when he returns, as Timon might have returned, to Athens, and is lord of the city.

The play ends in justice and reconciliation, and in this it might seem to be a forerunner of the Romances. Alcibiades returns to Athens, where, so he says, he 'will use the olive with the sword'. Misanthropy gives way to retribution and repentance; and in both Alcibiades and the Athenians themselves there is a change of heart which restores society for a while to peace and civil decency.

XLIV

Character seems, in a special sense, to be the fulfilment of vision in the women of the Romances. One of the most notable elements in all the Romances is the representation of innocent natural maidenhood—in Marina, Imogen, Perdita, and Miranda. These plays get much of their freshness from the unembarrassed virtue and candour of these girls. Perdita is as natural in her appetites as the ewes she milks and the flowers she wears in her hair. Miranda has a 'plain and holy innocence' which puts coyness and coquetry to shame.

A man, perhaps, in the autumn of his life, the flush of his days past, does not desire—unless there is a

pathological itch in his flesh—the return of spring or
summer merely for the renewal of his vigour. More than
all else he has a nostalgia for innocence. His years make
him guilty and what had once promised a hallowing
seems to have brought only a pollution. These portraits
of innocent girlhood may be thought to have something
of this nostalgia in them.

XLV

But the Romances present very puzzling problems,
as we can see from such diametrically opposed views as
those, say, of Lytton Strachey, who sees in them nothing
but fatigue, and of Dr. E. M. W. Tillyard, who believes
that they present the whole theme of the *Divine Comedy*.
My own argument will best proceed by a discussion of
Dr. Tillyard's view—and by examining this view in terms
of the relation between character and vision.

Dr. Tillyard disagrees with Sir Edmund Chambers
and with Lytton Strachey in their view that there is a
'profound cleavage in Shakespeare's mental history',
and that, after some kind of mental breakdown, in
the Romances Shakespeare made a new start, about
1607–8. Dr. Tillyard affirms, on the other hand, that the
Romances supplement the Tragedies, and that there is
a natural and unbroken development from the Tragedies
to the Romances. In other words, Dr. Tillyard believes
that in his final plays Shakespeare elaborates 'the closing
phase of the tragic pattern', the theme of regeneration,
the quickening of creative processes after the destructive
principle has done its worst.

Dr. Tillyard emphasizes his view by pointing out what he feels to be the distinction between true regeneration in *Othello* and a mere passing from one frame of mind, from one attitude to another, in *Antony and Cleopatra*. He suggests that in *Othello* there is a true educative and transforming process, while in *Antony and Cleopatra* the consummation does not spring from the chaos and destruction that have gone before. You might say that the reborn Othello would not make the mistakes of the old—although that is a mechanical way of thinking about the matter. You could not say this of Antony. 'In the same way,' Tillyard writes, 'Coriolanus's submission to his mother is a single act, however impressive, which involves no re-grouping, much less fusion and re-casting, of his previous qualities.'

In the Romances Tillyard believes that Shakespeare rediscovered the nature of regeneration, 'a melting down of the old vessel and a re-casting of it into something new'. So much is Tillyard seized of this view that in his Epilogue he writes:

It is almost as if (Shakespeare) aimed at rendering the complete theme of the *Divine Comedy*. Indeed, it is not fantastic to see in *The Winter's Tale* Shakespeare's attempt to compress the whole theme into a single play through the direct presentation of its parts: and it was with this notion in mind that I spoke of the country scenes as an earthly paradise. The motives of hell and purgatory in Leontes are obvious enough, while the statue scene is conducted in a rarefied atmosphere of contemplation that suggests the motive of paradise.

There is one preliminary comment to be made on

Tillyard's view concerning Shakespeare's mental history. Tillyard is at pains to reject Chambers's notion that Shakespeare experienced a sharp cleavage, perhaps a breakdown, some time after the composition of the great tragedies. He finds a consistent and 'unbroken' development from the tragedies to the Romances. It is difficult to see how, on his own showing, he sustains this view. In *Antony and Cleopatra* and in *Coriolanus*, Tillyard misses the true transforming and regenerative processes which are for him the marks of great tragedy. Antony and Cleopatra do not, according to Tillyard, suffer that chemical change of the spirit, from which health may return. If, then, in the Romances Shakespeare comes back to the sense of this re-quickening of life's processes after the destructive principle has worked itself out, there cannot be 'unbroken' development. For in the later Roman plays, according to Tillyard himself, this sense is lost. It would seem to me that there is in fact no break and that the development from the tragedies to the Romances is consistent and even—that there is a movement away from the emphasis on the validities of inner experience, the transforming as in a crucible of the chemistry of the spirit, to another view and vision, more social, more secular, a view already presiding over the composition of *Antony and Cleopatra* and *Coriolanus*.

If the Romances do indeed 'supplement' the tragedies in the way Tillyard suggests, then the characters in the Romances—or at least some of them—must have a like spiritual importance with those of the tragedies. Shakespeare could not render 'the entire theme of the *Divine*

Comedy' unless he also rendered in character the importance of the human spirit. And he cannot render the
importance of the human spirit, if his characters lack
spiritual concreteness. Now this is precisely what the
characters of the Romances—and I think especially of
the wicked persons of the plays—do lack. Evil in them is
quite opaque to goodness, and what they were before has
nothing to do with what they are after. What change is
wrought in them is effected merely by external agency,
and our interest in the change is not that it should have
happened within them, but that it should have happened
to them, and that, because of it, society is for the time
being cleansed and sweetened. But the cleansing and the
sweetening are not done either with humility or compassion. Even the forgiveness—of Hermione for Leontes,
of Prospero for Alonzo—has little compassion in it, and
in those forgiven there is submission, and a show of remorse, but no humility.

In Leontes we have very good evidence of the change
—it amounts almost to an impairment—in Shakespeare's vision, which is the key to our reading of the
Romances. We might even feel in the early part of the
play—perhaps Shakespeare felt it, too—that the writing
is a little stale, because Shakespeare had done it, or
something very like it, before. So much so, that there is
a certain morbidity in the representation of the state of
jealousy, and the effect is one of *pastiche*. Shakespeare's
craft was, of course, such that he was able to give to the
situation dramatic authority, but much is left to the
virtuosity of the actor. We are, indeed, hard put to it

to recognize the earlier Leontes in the later, and the remorse is never in poetry impregnated with the memory of earlier guilt. A 'sainted sorrow' hardly becomes the man who has done what Leontes has done, and what has happened within the repentant spirit is made altogether subordinate to the mere fact of repentance. That Leontes should repent and that Hermione should forgive are deductions from the theme of the play; and while forgiveness becomes more grateful and more gracious in Hermione, we know nothing more about the mysteries of repentance in Leontes. For these reasons Leontes is an acting part, rather than a character.

We have seen, in *King Lear*, how Shakespeare comes nearest to the creation of character within a 'kingdom of ends', which is itself an organic constituent of universal Nature. We are aware in *Lear*, though not perfectly, of a creative community of moral beings, in which the individual is at one and the same time the agent and the product of the society within which he has physical—and metaphysical—being. Society is not the sum but the integration of the individuals that compose it, and social order is the condition of individual moral being, individual moral being the determinant of social order. None of this, however, is true of the vision of the Romances, and none of it applies to the conception of character in the Romances. The characters of the Romances have status not in a metaphysical universe, but in society—a society that continues through the generations—and they mend their ways not in the sight of God, but in the sight of men. Not one of them is a

soul to be saved for its own sake, and social order seems
to require from them not creative moral being but submission, even obedience. They are under the Dispensation of the Law, and they have no part in the Covenant
of Grace. This is true even of Prospero, who has about
him not a little of a character from the Old Testament.

Perhaps this view seems not to apply to the women
of the Romances. It was, indeed, a long process from
'Frailty, thy name is Woman' to the sweet submissive-
ness of Hermione, to the fresh innocence of Perdita and
Miranda. But I am much mistaken if in Shakespeare's
creation of these women characters he reveals anything
of that spiritual importance which once he found in
men. They are, as Desdemona was, even Hermione, in
their innocence, like Eve before the Fall. They justify
Coleridge's words, when he says: 'all the elements of
womanhood are holy, and there is a sweet yet dignified
feeling of all that continuates society, as sense of ancestry
and sex.' That is surely the point. Woman's work is seen
as secular work. Woman never supposes that the spirit
might reach out to some 'infiniteness' and find there its
validity. The preoccupations of her goodness are thought
to be at the hearth, and in the home. Society is sweetened
by woman, not by communion, but by contagion, and it
is her function to 'continuate' and to conserve it.

Shakespeare leaves us in no doubt about his concern
with the relation between character and society, and in
the Romances he comes near to supposing that character
is a product of social and natural environment. Or if, by
some strange chance, goodness and innocence are found

in an evil society, it cannot stay there, it will be expelled
or go into exile, and it will return only when, by some
means of punishment or explanation, the members of
that society have seen the evil in themselves and have
repented. The influence of environment is mentioned
explicitly, and there is a ring of something more than
mere conventionalism in the passage when Belarius in
Cymbeline contrasts the life of courts with the life of the
mountains and the caves:

> O, this life
> Is nobler than attending for a check,
> Richer than doing nothing for a bauble,
> Prouder than rustling in unpaid-for silk:
> Such gain the cap of him that makes 'em fine,
> Yet keeps his books uncross'd; no life to ours.

Perdita and Miranda might well have been in Wordsworth's mind when he wrote:

> Three years she grew in sun and shower.
> Then Nature said, 'A lovelier flower
> On earth was never sown;
> This Child I to myself will take,
> She shall be mine, and I will make
> A Lady of my own.'

Not only Nature, however, has made them what they
are—and this is true, too, of the boys in *Cymbeline*—but
the royalty which they 'continuate' from the society
whence they sprung, and from which they were sent into
exile.

For in an evil society, goodness seems to have no

choice but to go into exile until Time brings its revenges and repentances. This, indeed, is the pattern of the Romances. So, in *Pericles*, the Prince must wander from place to place, always away from Tyre; in *Cymbeline*, Posthumus is sent to Rome, and Imogen is first kept prisoner and then escapes to the cave; in *The Winter's Tale*, Hermione is secluded for sixteen years; and in *The Tempest*, Prospero and Miranda are set adrift in a little boat by a wicked kinsman in Milan. Do we not find this pattern already anticipated in *Timon of Athens*, where the city proves unworthy both of Timon and of Alcibiades?

XLVI

Time and the accidents of Time bring order again into society, and through Time goodness comes into its own. When Posthumus is asked what means he makes to win the king again, he answers:

> Not any; but abide the change of time;
> Quake in the present winter's state, and wish
> That warmer days would come.

Hermione and Prospero both have to wait until a propitious time before they can return to the world they had abandoned, and it is, as it were, an accident that makes the time propitious—for Hermione must wait until Perdita comes back to Sicily, and Prospero must wait until the king's ship is within his range of power.

The most notable 'change of time' is the change of generations, and Shakespeare's concern with society is a concern not merely with social order, but also with social continuance. In the Middle Comedies we may detect, perhaps, what is one of the secrets of Comedy—I mean the conflict between that Reason which sustains the principle of social order and those appetites which in one way or another are necessary to social continuance. Love makes men foolish, but without Love how should the world go on? In the Romances, where towards youth especially a more nostalgic attitude prevails, those energies and appetites by which society is continuated receive different and more explicit treatment. Dr. Tillyard, and others, have made a great deal of the fertility-symbols in the Romances and find in them images of spiritual renewal. Had that more general criticism, which relates character to vision, guided the more particular, which interests itself a little too mechanically in symbols, it would have observed that the conception of character in the Romances cannot sustain the notion of spiritual renewal, but that the notion of the renewal of the generations, mother and daughter, father and son, of biological renewal, social continuance, is everywhere proclaimed. Hermione's pregnancy; the candour of Perdita; the unabashed innocence of Miranda; the prodigality of Nature in the spring-time; the warmth of the sun in May; all these are symbols of that sweet vigour in young men and women which enables the succession of the generations.

Nor in all this should we forget that puzzling Puritanism in Prospero—puzzling, perhaps, but not to be lightly dismissed—which makes him warn Ferdinand and Miranda more than once:

> If thou dost break her virgin knot before
> All sanctimonious ceremonies may
> With full and holy rite be minister'd,
> No sweet aspersion shall the heavens let fall
> To make this contract grow.

For the continuance of society is now at one with social order, and they are involved in each other, and in Time. We should respect Shakespeare's seriousness in the statement of this view, however much the ceremonial occasion for *The Tempest* may have here endorsed it. The harmony between what had once been seen as opposites—between that Reason which makes for order and those appetites which enable continuance—is the major reconciliation, amongst so many others, in the Romances.

XLVII

To present the continuance of society through the generations was also to present character in a deeper perspective. And, as we look back on the relationship between character and vision in Shakespeare's plays, we recognize that time and time's perspectives, in so far as these are primary disciplines in Shakespeare's art, afford a clue to the development of that art. Time, after all, is as much the playwright's discipline as space is the painter's, and as the painter may work many kinds of perspective in space, so the playwright must work many kinds of perspective in time. In these perspectives vision fulfils itself in character.

In the Romances, Shakespeare's vision comes to a certain settlement with 'calumniating time'; and the serenity, the acceptance, which mark the vision of the Romances is partly, at least, a matter of time-perspective. The Romances are plays in which the relationship between the generations is seen as a relationship in time, and, from one generation to the other, time is seen as the dimension in which wounds may be healed and life renewed. Time is accepted as the destroyer, because time is also the agent of renewal.

This view of time requires that we should not be too close to the moment of destruction, and that we should feel much of the sweetness, little of the agony, of the moment of renewal. In the Romances, then, it is as though we are looking at what happens in time through the wrong end of a time-telescope, and Shakespeare presents his characters, as it were, in deep focus. It is for this reason that in the Romances all the characters are, in a sense, minor characters, for, being removed from the centre of vision, they lack the depths of psychological perspective and they lack in themselves the immediacy of moral importance, which a closer apperception might have afforded them. They have, in drawing, the sharpness and the simplicity of a miniature, and it is this which makes *The Tempest*, of all Shakespeare's plays, the most suitable for presentation in a theatre of puppets. It is this, too, which makes the essential difference between Iachimo and Iago.

This settlement with Time has, too, its more sombre aspect in the Romances. The generations see not only the renewal of life, but also the passing of life into the anonymity of death:

> Golden lads and lasses must
> As chimney-sweepers come to dust.

And when Prospero says:

> We are such stuff
> As dreams are made on, and our little life
> Is rounded with a sleep,

he reports truly of the vision which is fulfilled by character in the remoter time-perspective of Shakespeare's
last plays.

INDEX OF NAMES

Achilles, 127, 129, 133.
Ajax, 127.
Albany, 119.
Alchemist, The, 19.
Alcibiades, 132, 133, 141.
Alexander, Peter, 123, 127, 130, 131.
Alexas, 21.
Alonzo, 64, 65, 137.
Alving, Mrs., 11.
Angelo, 11, **67–72**.
Antonio, 22, 41, 43, 74.
Antony and Cleopatra, 20, 81, **122–6**, 129, 135, 136.
Antony, 79, 80, **122–6**, 127, 129, 135, 136.
Apemantus, 130, 132.
Aragon, Prince of, 43.
Aristotle, 4, 90.
Arthur, 45.
Aumerle, 48.
Autolycus, 15.

Banquo, 102, 104.
Barnardine, 20.
Bassanio, 13, 41, 42, 43.
Bastard, The, 28.
Belarius, 140.
Bennet, Elizabeth, 66.
Bolingbroke (*see* Henry IV), 45, 50.
Boswell, James, 26.
Brabantio, 92.
Bridges, Robert, 7, 68.
Brutus, 45, **53–56**.
Burgundy, 112.

Caesar and Cleopatra, 49.
Caesar, Julius, 55.
Caesar, Octavius, 122, 123.
Carlyle, Thomas, 109.

Cassio, 12, 97.
Cassius, 56.
Chambers, E. K., 134, 136.
— R. W., 67.
Chaplin, Charlie, 16.
Charmian, 21.
Churchill, Winston, 50.
Claudio, 72.
Cleopatra, 20, 21, **122–6**, 127, 136.
Clytemnestra, 11.
Cocktail Party, The, 38, 39.
Coleridge, S. T., 2, 15, 18, 42, 57, 139.
Cominius, 127.
Corbaccio, 19, 20.
Cordelia, 17, **60–63**, 112, 113, 114, 116.
Coriolanus, 81, **122–6**, 129, 136.
Coriolanus, 11, 79, 80, 122–6, 127, 128, 132, 135.
Cornwall, Duke of, 113.
Corvino, 19.
Cressida, 127.
Cymbeline, 140, 141.

Danby, J. F., 60–63.
Darcy, Fitzwilliam, 66.
Desdemona, 17, 92, 95, 139.
Diomed, 127.
Divine Comedy, 134, 135, 136.
Dolabella, 127.
Dostoievsky, 120.
Dromios, The, 24.
Duncan, 76, 98, 99, 100, 102, 104, 107.

Edgar, 109, 113, 114.
Edmund, 22, 110, 113, 115, 116, 118, 119.

Eliot, T. S., 8, 13, 38, 106, 118, 119.
Emilia, 12, 93.
Enobarbus, 21.

Falstaff, 4, 5, **13–15,** 17, **35–36,** 49, 50, 51, 75, 82, 83, 125.
Ferdinand, 142.
Fool (*Lear*), 33, 89.
France, King of, 112, 115.
Freud, Sigmund, 6.

Garrick, David, 1.
Gertrude, 11, 111.
Glendower, Owen, 47.
Gloucester, Duchess of, 48.
— Earl of, 17, 109, 113, 116, 117, 119.
Gobbo, 74.
Goneril, 112, 115, 116, 119.
Gratiano, 42.

Hamlet, 23, **56–59,** 77, 79, 111.
Hamlet, 1, 2, 5, 11, 23, **33–34, 56–59,** 76, 77, 79, 106, 111.
Hedda Gabler, 39.
Hedda Gabler, 39.
Henry IV, Parts I and II, 35.
Henry IV (*see* Bolingbroke), 51.
Henry V, 50.
Henry V, 13, 36, 45, 46, 49, 50, 51, 74.
Hermione, 6, 65, 137, 138, 139, 141, 142.
Holinshed, 49.
Horatio, 77.
Hotspur, 27, 29, 47, 50.
Hubert, 45.

Iachimo, 65, 133, 144.
Iago, 4, 12, 15, 19, 22, 27, 28, **30–33,** 34, 81, 87, **92–97,** 108, 144.

Ibsen, Henrik, 39.
Imogen, 133, 141.
Iras, 21.

Jaques, 15.
Jessica, 42.
Jocasta, 11.
Johnson, Samuel, 1, 26.
Jones, Ernest, 10, 57.
Jonson, Ben, 19, 130, 131.
Julia, 37.
Juliet, 17.
Julius Caesar, 53, 54.

Keats, John, 2, 8, 15.
Kemble, J. P., 1.
Kent, 17, 112, 113, 114, 116, 132.
King Lear, 33, **60–63,** 76, 78, 79, 98, **108–20,** 125, 132, 138.
Knight, G. Wilson, 92.

Lady Macbeth, 7, 98, 99, 100–3.
Laertes, 57.
Launce, 24, 25.
Launcelot Gobbo, 4, 24, 25, 43, 74.
Lear, 17, 22, 33, 61, 76, 78, 79, 83, 84–85, 89, **108–20,** 125, 132.
Lennox, 99.
Leontes, **6–8,** 10, 64, 65, 135, 137, 138.
Lorenzo, 42, 44.
Lucio, 66, 69, 70.

Macbeth, 7, 77, 91–92, **97–108,** 125.
Macbeth, 7, 9, 69, 70, 76, 78, 88, **97–108,** 125.
Malvolio, 17, 36, 75, 82, 83.
Marcellus, 77.
Marina, 133.
Measure for Measure, 20, **66–72,** 92.
Merchant of Venice, The, 22, **40–44,** 87, 92.

Mercutio, 23–24, 28, 34.
Miranda, 133, 139, 140, 141, 142.
Morgann, Maurice, 13.
Morocco, Prince of, 42.
Morozov, M. M., 28, 30, 33.
Moscha, 19.

Nerissa, 42.
Northumberland, Earl of, 47.
Nurse (*R. and J.*), 24.

Oedipus, 11.
Ophelia, 17, 34, 111.
Orestes, 11.
Orsino, 22, 74.
Oswald (*Ghosts*), 11.
— (*Lear*), 113.
Othello, 12, 13, **91–97,** 106, 107, 108, 125, 135.
Othello, 4, 12, 27, 28, **30–33,** 40, 76, 77, 78, 79, 80, 87, **91–97,** 108, 125, 135.

Perdita, 133, 139, 140, 141, 142.
Pericles, 141.
Plutarch, 49, 53.
Polixenes, 6, 8.
Portia, 13, 41, 42, 43, 44.
Posthumus, 141.
Prospero, 65, 129, 137, 139, 141, 142, 145.
Proteus, 37.

Regan, 109, 112.
Richard II, 47, 48, 50, 53.
Richard II, 45, 51.
— III, 1, 15, 19.
Roderigo, 92.
Romeo, 17, 23, 24.
Rymer, Thomas, 13, 50.

Saint Joan, 49.

Salanio, 41.
Salarino, 40, 41.
Schücking, L. L., 54.
Seneca, 119, 120.
Shaw, Bernard, 49, 128, 129.
Shylock, 36, 42, 43, 75, 82, 83.
Silvia, 37.
Stewart, J. I. M., 2, 6, 7, 20, 54, 55, 68, 69, 106.
Stoll, E. E., 57.
Strachey, Lytton, 134.

Tarleton, Richard, 25.
Tempest, The, 8, 64, 141, 143, 144.
Tesman, 39.
Thersites, 130, 132.
Tillyard, E. M. W., 40, 134, 135, 136, 142.
Timon of Athens, 81, **129–33,** 141.
Timon, 80, **129–33,** 141.
Troilus and Cressida, **126–9,** 130, 132.
Twelfth Night, 22, 74.
Two Gentlemen of Verona, The, 36.
Tybalt, 23.

Ulysses, 127, 129.

Valentine, 37.
Vienna, Duke of, 72.
Volpone, **19–20,** 130–1.
Volpone, 19, 20, 131.
Voltore, 19.
Volumnia, 11, 135.

Waste Land, The, 118.
Winter's Tale, The, 6, 10, 60, 135, 141.
Worcester, Earl of, 47.
Wordsworth, William, 140.

Yorick, 77.
York, Duke of, 47, 48, 53.
— Duchess of, 48.